FUTURE MINDED

FUTURE MINDED

PREPARING TODAY'S YOUTH
FOR TOMORROW'S WORKPLACE

ZAIMAH KHAN

NEW DEGREE PRESS

FUTURE MINDED
Preparing Today's Youth for Tomorrow's Workplace

ISBN   978-1-64137-993-9 *Paperback*
                 978-1-64137-893-2 *Kindle Ebook*
                 978-1-64137-894-9 *Ebook*

Education is the passport to the future, for tomorrow belongs to those who prepare for it today.

MALCOLM X

For Rehan and Aidin.

*Every day with you is a new adventure, and without
you two I wouldn't have embarked on this quest.*

To Sonny, thank you for your love and support in all my endeavors.

*To my parents, siblings, and my chosen family, it is your love,
prayers, and wisdom that have made me into the woman I am.*

CONTENTS

INTRODUCTION

———

When my older son was about ten years old, he said that he wanted to be a *"YouTuber"* when he grew up. We had already cycled through the usual job options that most little boys want. He wanted to be a policeman, a fireman, a teacher, a cashier at Target, a soccer player, and numerous other positions. My son, like many other young children, is part of the generation that enjoys watching others play video games, so he wanted to start his own channel, play his video games, and get enough subscribers so he could be a YouTube celebrity.

"What kind of jobs will my kids have?" was a question that had been percolating in my head ever since my kids were born in the oughts. Then in 2012, I had a *"mind-blown"* kind of year because of three momentous events. First, my oldest started Kindergarten. Second, I started another master's degree program. Third, I heard Sir Ken Robinson's speech on shifting education paradigms, which made me reevaluate everything I knew about teaching. Given that I was a teacher at a community college and that my son was starting Kindergarten, hearing Sir Ken Robinson describe the history of

why schools are organized the way they are, and they are still run the way they used to be over a century ago made me rethink my question from *"what kind of jobs will my kids have?"* to *"how do you prepare kids for jobs that don't exist yet?"* when they're learning in a system designed for a different world.

Nearly four years later when my son, declared he wanted to be a YouTuber, my immediate gut reaction was *"Hell no!"* but when I stopped to think about how much the world has changed and what the future could hold for my sons and kids of their generation...YouTuber is a reasonable occupation. It is becoming more and more evident that the old career template that we had been directed to follow is not what's going to take us into the future. In the past, a four-year college degree was a guarantee of employability. It meant a way to support a family. It was enough and, for the most part, it also meant the end of formal learning in preparation for a job. Those of us who are in our mid-careers witnessed our parents follow this model and can probably recall moments from our youth when we were told that a four-year college degree was the pathway to success. We have harbored those same expectations for our children. However, things in 2020 are very different than they were in 1990.

In 2016, Klaus Schwab, Founder and Executive Chairman of the World Economic Forum wrote[1]:

---

1   Klaus Schwab, "The Fourth Industrial Revolution: What It Means and How to Respond."

"We stand on the brink of a technological revolution that will fundamentally alter the way we live, work, and relate to one another. In its scale, scope, and complexity, the transformation will be unlike anything humankind has experienced before."

We are entering an age of artificial intelligence and robots in the workplace. The way that we work has changed. Things like what does an office look like, or where you work from, and how you work have changed from the nine to five mindset. Career paths are no longer about rising through the ranks in a specific company or a single industry but more about a life path as work-life balance gives way to work-life integration, and people are seeking jobs that provide them personal and professional fulfillment. We have longer life spans and because there's no longer the concept of staying at a company long enough to earn a pension, so more people are having to or looking at staying in the workforce longer.

"The outdated industrial-age mindset where people received an education early in life to be ready for a lifetime of work no longer reflects the individualized and unexpected trajectories of modern careers."[2]

WORLD ECONOMIC FORUM

---

2   Simon Fuglsang Østergaard and Adam Graafland Nordlund, "The 4 Biggest Challenges to Our Higher Education Model—and What to Do About Them."

After several declarations of my son's desire to be a YouTuber, my husband and I were forced to confront our prejudices about the old path of school, to college, and to work. We had an earnest conversation about how our template of life and learning might not be our kids' exact path. Especially since he and I, and those of us in mid-career have already had to re-skill and up-skill and look at our careers with a new lens, and even switch career paths or industries. In fact, my cousin's best friend graduated from Georgetown with an accounting and finance degree. She worked in accounting, went into consulting, and now is the COO of a company that analyzes and updates HVAC systems. She speaks about LEED certification and WELL certification with such passion and animation that when I ask her if she could have imagined that this was what would excite her when she graduated from college, the answer was a resounding no.

Those of us in the workforce are already making changes toward these non-linear career paths. Given how quickly things are evolving, I can't help question what will be my children's experience?

- What will be the jobs when they graduate college?
- What will be the jobs five to ten years after that?
- Will they be prepared?

As a former educator and a current organization development and human capital specialist, people development is my area of expertise. I know that currently there is a workforce skills gap in soft skills, or people skills. And as we move into an age of automation and artificial intelligence, our soft skills—our uniquely human skills—are what will help *us and our kids* succeed because in the Fourth Industrial Revolution what can be done by a machine will be—jobs that can be automated will become automated. We find ourselves at a point in history where:

- the world is different and will be even more so in the Fourth Industrial Revolution because of automation and artificial intelligence;
- career paths are no longer linear, rather they curve, and wind around as new opportunities and options are created;
- the skills we all need to succeed in the Fourth Industrial Revolution are our uniquely human skills, but employers say that those skills are missing in today's workforce,
- and our kids continue to be taught in an educational system that hasn't changed in over a hundred years and has greatly contributed to the skills gap.

Thereby, begging the question:

Why have we reached the Fourth Industrial Revolution in work, but our teaching model has remained largely the same as it was during the First Industrial Revolution?

Our education system needs a major overhaul because the United States education system has not changed since the end of the nineteenth century when single-room schoolhouses began opening across the country in greater numbers. The Department of Education was created in 1867 to help collect information from the various schools to create a public education system, and while the schools have evolved from the one room, one teacher teaching reading, writing, and arithmetic to all ages, the curriculum and systems haven't significantly changed. Schools are still largely a place to teach kids to be prepared to be compliant, something that was necessary to prepare them for a life of working in factories in a world that has evolved beyond factory jobs.

The education system needs to be forward thinking and look at the skills and knowledge that our youth need to succeed in an age of robots and machines. As we move into the Fourth Industrial Revolution, there are already significant shifts in the type of work and jobs that exist, yet our school curriculum has not evolved enough to fulfill the needs of the workplace. And while I would like for us to say let's scrap the current educational models we have and start fresh, that is not and cannot be the reality, so we need to find innovative ways to work with what we have.

So, with past templates becoming obsolete what do we as parents, educators, and leaders do to prepare future generations?

Based on research from the World Economic Foundation, other leading companies, and interviews with business leaders, I found that there are certain skills that are *always* in demand in the workforce and will continue to be in demand for the future of work. The skills can be divided into two sets.

The first set of skills are related to developing one's self:

1. Emotional Intelligence
2. Resilience
3. Adaptability
4. Critical Thinking
5. Complex Problem-Solving

The second set of skills are related to interacting with others:

6. Empathy
7. Negotiation
8. Teamwork
9. Conflict Resolution

These nine skills show up in different ways in business. They may not be listed on job descriptions or resumés, but in nearly every interview I conducted these were the ones that were mentioned as being needed now and for the future of work. It may be surprising that none of these relate to academics, and instead they relate to the overall traits or personality of individuals. It isn't about academics versus character. Ultimately what many people have emphasized in research and experience, teaching people how to program robots is much easier than teaching them to care about their co-workers. Alvin Toffler, author of *Future Shock* wrote[3]:

"The illiterate of the 21st century will not be those who cannot read and write, but those who cannot learn, unlearn, and relearn."

Until now, going to school and finishing a four-year degree have been the steps to employment and are ingrained in the heads of parents, teachers, and really the whole society. But as Toffler predicted half a century ago, in the twenty-first century career paths will require the workforce to engage in lifelong learning. To be skilling, re-skilling, and up-skilling to stay competitive and employed. As proof of his words is

---

3   Alvin Toffler, *Oxford Essential Quotations*, ed. Susan Ratcliffe.

the fact that we seem to be playing catch up in workforce skills. First it was STEM skills, then it was the addition of art, so STEAM skills only to discover that we were falling behind in the soft skills. We are two decades into the century, and instead of being ready, we're still trying to get caught up rather than preparing future generations.

All of this is not to say that school or college is not important and that degrees will become obsolete, but we cannot rely on systems that were designed for a time period that looks very different than what we're in and where we're heading. Lifelong learning is the way forward, and the human skills that I have identified, provide parents, teachers, and leaders with the essential skills that will serve our children best in their non-linear career paths. Paths that will require adopting the mindset of lifelong learning because they will need to up-skill, re-skill frequently, and they must be able to do it effectively and efficiently.

CHAPTER 1:

THE FUTURE OF WORK

"(There is an) increasing need for life-long learning in a non-linear world."

WORLD ECONOMIC FORUM[4]

Twenty-ish years ago when I graduated from college, my college's career services advisor told me that I could expect to have up to eight jobs and two different career paths during my work life. At that time, it seemed like a radical deviation from the notion that a person worked for one company his whole life, and retired with a pension from that company. Even though it wasn't. Interestingly, many people in the business world still write about shattering this model, as if it's the norm even though it stopped being the norm in the 1990s

---

4   Simon Fuglsang Østergaard and Adam Graafland Nordlund, "The 4 biggest challenges to our higher education model—and what to do about them."

as private sector pensions started sharply declining.[5] Today, about halfway into my workforce trajectory of forty-ish years of work that template has been smashed to smithereens. I have worked for nine different companies and have held over fourteen jobs, since the start of my professional career, and if I include all the jobs I have held during my lifetime, that number would double.

At the time when I graduated from college, work meant gaining a nine to five job or some variation of a forty-hour work week. A workplace was somewhere you went during work hours and did your job. You received standard benefits of ten days' time-off. If you got more than that or paid sick leave, then it was a really good job. A career path meant finding a field or industry that you were passionate about and working your way up to the top of it. A bachelor's degree was sufficient but eventually a master's degree could be helpful on the road to the top.

"The very notion of "work," "workplace," and "career" has evolved significantly since the start of the 21st century."

At the time of my college graduation, I don't think we could have imagined how different the workplace would look in twenty years—in terms of types of jobs like app developer, influencer, cloud computing, or smart house engineer. We could not have fathomed that remote work and collaborative work spaces would be the norm—rather than a brick and mortar presence—or that the definition of a *"career"* would become a path of learning and working; the skills

---

5   Tyler Bond, "What Happened to Private Sector Pensions?"

and experience that a person possesses because we would shift from work-life balance to work-life integration. Now in my forties, when I look around and take stock of my career, I find myself thinking about my kids' future. I am in awe of the new industries and types of jobs that have been created and the way things are heading in the *future of work*.

What does it mean to be prepared for the future of work?

First off, let's define some of the jargon because the uncertainty about the future also has to do with all the jargon that is thrown around, which makes the unknown a lot more daunting than it already is. Deloitte defines the *future of work* as "*the growing adoption of artificial intelligence in the workplace, and the expansion of the workforce to include both on-and off-balance-sheet talent*" where on-balance-sheet talent means company employees and off-balance-sheet means freelancers, contractors, or temporary workers.[6]

Then we have the term the Fourth Industrial Revolution. Many of us remember learning about the industrial revolution in school and have a vague idea of it being toward the end of the eighteenth or start of the nineteenth century. We associate it with the invention of the steam engine and mass production of goods. Historians, however, have over time refined the industrial periods. In the United States, the First Industrial Revolution was at the tail end of the eighteenth century with the introduction of steam power, industrialization, urbanization, and mechanical manufacturing. The Second Industrial Revolution was toward the end of the

---

6   Deloitte Insights, "Future of Work."

nineteenth century and start of the twentieth century and is marked by mass production, assembly lines, and widespread adoption of early technology like the telegraph and transportation. The Third Industrial Revolution started in the latter half of the twentieth century and is related to Internet technology, renewable energy, and information and communications technology.

This brings us to the Fourth Industrial Revolution, the age of robotics, artificial intelligence, the Internet of things, digitalization, and automation.[7] Some pundits say that we are in the Fourth Industrial Revolution, whereas others say that we're at the brink of it. Based on the industries that have been transformed, it would be safe to assume we're already in it; eventually maybe thirty years or so from now will pinpoint a more accurate time as the start of this next era. Another business term that is often associated with the *future of work* and the Fourth Industrial Revolution is Industry 4.0, and sometimes the terms Fourth Industrial Revolution and Industry 4.0 are used interchangeably.[8] But, Industry 4.0 is a specific subcategory in the Fourth Industrial Revolution that refers *only* to the industries that are evolving and not any other aspects of the Fourth Industrial Revolution.

In the past decade, Industry 4.0 has begun to take shape with advancement and acceleration of use in cloud computing, automation, artificial intelligence, cognitive computing, and

7   Armstrong, et al, "Preparing Tomorrow's Workforce for the Fourth Industrial Revolution. For business: A framework for Action."

8   Bernard Marr, "What is Industry 4.0? Here's a Super Easy Explanation for Anyone."

the Internet of things.[9] It builds on trends like automation in manufacturing and technological processes that started during Industry 3.0. Industry 4.0 includes the Internet of Things and the Internet of Systems, which make the smart factory possible —factories that are more efficient, productive, and less wasteful. The societal changes that have come about, and will continue to occur because these manufacturing and technological advances are what will make up the Fourth Industrial Revolution.

Artificial intelligence is a significant part of what is advancing Industry 4.0. Though there are a range of definitions of what artificial intelligence is, Artificial intelligence is best thought of as an entire field of study oriented around developing computing systems capable of performing tasks that otherwise would require human intelligence, like mobile check deposits or voice assistants like Siri and Alexa.[10] The rise of these technologies has also brought up questions regarding the future of work, and what the jobs of the future look like, especially since according to the Society for Human Resource Management Skills Gap 2019 report, states that *"seventy-five percent of those involved in recruiting say that there is a shortage of skills."*[11]

The skills gap in the workforce right now exists because we are still using past education systems and models for what life looked like, not how it is now or will look like. Our education models are from a different time. Once upon a time

---

9   Ibid.

10   Rob Toews, "What Does 'Artificial Intelligence' Really Mean?"

11   Society for Human Resource Management, "The Skills Gap 2019."

a four-year college degree was the path to a stable job from which you could retire with a pension. The last generation where that template has truly worked is the baby boomers who are now retiring or close to it. In the Fourth Industrial Revolution, we will need to figure out ways to navigate through change quickly and efficiently. However, we can't do that by following models of years past. Gen Xers are in their mid to late-mid careers. The oldest Gen Xer is still a few years away from retirement, and the oldest millennials are reaching their mid-career points. To be successful in the new era of work, we need to think about our own professional journey, and we need to rethink the way that we teach and prepare our youth for the workforce.

Shifting work paradigms mean that skills are becoming the currency of the labor market, and this is shifting the importance of the traditional path of college education.[12] Along with rising college tuition prices, crippling college student debt, and students graduating from college and unable to find jobs that pay them enough for them to become independent, people are questioning the value of the traditional path to college. As a college instructor, I witnessed this tension in my students who were anxious to learn the *"tangible skills"* they needed to get out in the workforce. The mindset was increasingly shifting toward education that provided a clear path to employment, and so for them, the ESL student who had to take academic English classes, general education courses, and major courses. They were often frustrated. Classroom sentiment increasingly became *"teach me what I need to know, so I can move on."* Sean Hinton, Founder and

---

12   Østergaard, "The 4 Biggest Challenges to Our Higher Education Model."

CEO of Skyhive wrote, *"students are less interested in stale curriculums and keener to take shorter, skills-based training that is more relevant to today's workplace."*[13]

A degree is still useful and needed, but many employers are looking beyond academic qualifications, and some major companies are shifting from college degrees as a basic requirement. During the past decade, company emphasis has been on finding skilled workers, and what employers have found is that the workforce is coming up short. A definitive skills gap has been found, but what are the skills that we are short on right now? Human skills, aka soft skills. This is somewhat alarming as we enter the Fourth Industrial Revolution especially because as work becomes more automated and technologically advances, the jobs that are left behind are *"generally more interpretive and service-oriented, involving problem-solving, data interpretation, communications and listening, customer service and empathy, and teamwork and collaboration."*[14]

The term VUCA (volatility, uncertainty, chaos, ambiguity) is ubiquitously used nowadays to describe the workplace. Companies are going through rapid changes, and employees are feeling change fatigue. It seems that just as things are even keeled, a new change occurs. People are becoming tired of re-skilling and up-skilling because according to the template that we have been told or been following, college was the end of formal learning. People have been quick to blame

---

13   Sean Hinton, "How the Fourth Industrial Revolution is Impacting the Future of Work."

14   Volini, et al., "From Jobs to Superjobs."

technology for the crisis of poor soft skills. The reality is that the skills gap has been there for a while. It's there because, according to a Brookings Institute report, *"there is a lack of specificity in terms of what and how soft skills should be taught in the first place, which makes it incredibly difficult for teachers to incorporate them into curricula built to transfer hard skills."*[15]

The emphasis on professional development in recent years has encouraged some to adopt a more lifelong learning approach but many people are still hanging on to the past. Look at the people of the coal industry! Coal mining was a transformative industry during the First Industrial Revolution. Its merger with steel and rail created more opportunities in the Second Industrial Revolution. We, however, are poised at the start of the Fourth Industrial Revolution, and politicians are still pandering to the coal lobby. These are people whose skill sets are limited to an outdated and outmoded industry. Those who demand that there should be jobs created for them. Instead of betting on themselves and seeing the declining trajectory of coal mining, such workers doubled down on trying to hold on to an archaic type of work. Why? They're clinging to a past lifepath template that no longer works.

If we don't adapt either by entering industries where there are workforce shortages (or projected shortages) then we will need to adapt by acquiring the skills that the employers want, otherwise we will be left behind. People are scared about

---

15 Bridging the Soft Skills Gap.

automation and artificial intelligence. So many questions are asked surrounding the future like:

- What jobs will be automated?
- How many jobs will be lost?
- How many jobs will be created?

The good news is that each industrial revolution has brought more jobs than it has taken away.[16] The other side of this news is that the new jobs that are created will require a shift in skill sets, which will necessitate up-skilling and re-skilling of the workforce. Right now, employers are looking to colleges and universities to improve employee readiness in soft skills. There have been task forces between industry, government, and higher education to close the skills gaps but in looking to win the battle, we're overlooking the strategy to win the war.

I love learning. I am a student at heart. I treat educational institutions as hallowed ground. However, t's becoming more evident each day that things need to change in the education system. During the Third Industrial Revolution, talks of hard technical skills gaps began emerging as the US was being left behind in Science, Technology, Engineering, and Mathematics (STEM), educationally and professionally. Since the 1960s and 70s, the United States have been importing doctors and engineers from overseas to keep up with the skills needed.

---

16 Jayant Menon, "Why the Fourth Industrial Revolution Could Spell More Jobs—Not Fewer."

So, in the early 2000s, there was a massive curriculum shift toward STEM subjects. Then, in the decade following the 2010s, there was a push toward incorporating art turning STEM to STEAM: science, technology, engineering, art, and mathematics. Meanwhile over the past few years, employers have been discovering that while employees are technically capable in their jobs, they are lacking the soft skills, aka human skills, that are needed to flourish in the workplace. With all the focus on academics and constantly being tested on that knowledge, the academic focus of schools had taken away the skills that made humans–human.

Unfortunately, the timing of the soft skills gap has coincided with the millennials' rise in the workplace. So in some ways, soft skills weakness has become synonymous with a millennial weakness. However, it's not a generational flaw. Their generation came to adulthood during a recession, so they had difficulties finding jobs or worked in jobs where they were very underemployed. Add that to the fact that many millennials graduated with large amounts of college loan debt, which has led the millennial generation to rely on financial help from their parents. They will be the first generation that will earn less than their parents over their lifetime.

Millennials came of age in a different time not only because of the recession but also because the nature of work was changing. Yet, they were brought up with the life template of finishing Kindergarten through twelfth grade education, earning a college degree, and then getting a job. Many employers complained about their generation not being as prepared as previous generations, but what we need to do is take a step back and look at this generation that has been subject to excessive standardized testing, in addition to being over-parented and over-scheduled.

According to the US Chamber of Commerce 2017 Report on *Bridging the Soft Skills Gap*,[17] *"despite U.S. high school graduation rates reaching all-time highs, a growing number of employers across industries are reporting that job applicants lack the basic skills needed to succeed in the workforce. Even when applicants make it past the interview process, employers are coping with new hires who are unsure of how to write a professional email, struggle to organize and prioritize tasks, or have a difficult time collaborating with coworkers."* As *TIME* magazine notes, *"the entry-level candidates who are on tap to join the ranks of full-time work are clueless about the fundamentals of office life."* Somewhere along the road from education to employment, the system is not routinely equipping all students with all the skills they need to succeed.

These ever-changing skills gaps illustrate that we are chasing or trying to catch up with preparing our youth for the workforce. The purpose of education isn't solely to prepare for work, but that education is part of it.

We're entering the age of automation and artificial intelligence, and our school systems have been set up to prepare our children for the assembly lines. It's no wonder that we find ourselves in a situation where we are having to compensate for past gaps, but because we're looking back, we're not ready for the future. A recent Harvard Business Review

17   Bridging the Soft Skills Gap.

article, *To Prepare for Automation, Stay Curious and Don't Stop Learning*, the author Tiger Tyagarajan states three key things that must occur for us to thrive through the Fourth Industrial Revolution[18]:

- America will need to invest in new avenues of education and adopt a commitment to approaching education flexibly.
- Executives will need to be better about *"walking the walk"* when it comes to re-skilling existing employees whose current roles are destined to change.
- As a country, we need to better invest in our educational system while simultaneously embracing a culture of continuous and life-long learning.

Our education system's design is more than one hundred years old and that is the root of all the problems we have with schooling. Note, that I say system because it's not the teachers or even a particular school or school district that is flawed. It's how we think of education overall. We need to leave the mindset of desks and lectures and even group. Education is not just preparation for the real world but also where we learn how to learn, learn how to live, learn how to be part of a community, and learn how to be a citizen. Academic knowledge is not the only objective of education and it's time we reevaluated the way things are structured. We can't expect people to grow and evolve with a lifelong learning mindset, if we're forcing them to fit into particular templates. Moreover, if employers are going to hold the

---

18 Tiger Tyagarajan, "To Prepare for Automation, Stay Curious and Don't Stop Learning."

expectation that employees will continually up-skill and re-skill for different responsibilities and evolving job roles, then they're going to need to demonstrate similar attitudes and mindsets. Too often we see leadership place demands on their employees and expect compliance with whatever new idea or new technology they want to implement and not follow through on their own ideas.

Our teacher education programs recognize that students have different learning styles and emphasize preparing for a diverse classroom and to differentiate learning so that teachers reach all types of students. Research has indicated how the change in hormones during puberty impact that circadian rhythms and sleep cycles of teens. So, some school districts have changed their timings. Distance learning is on the rise. We're making changes as we learn new information, but we're making them in smaller increments. We need to look at the problem more broadly. We know that people aren't the same hence why standardized tests, or other such techniques of standardization don't work.

We also know that people learn differently. So, to *"learn and unlearn"* as Toffler said we need to rethink of what it means to school our youth. The IBM updated Buckminster Fuller Knowledge Doubling curve estimates that in 2020, knowledge will be doubled every twelve hours[19]. So, we all need to contend with more and more information, but at the same time, we will need to also determine which knowledge is valuable to retain over the long-term, and which information is best suited for a short time. And, if those of us

19   Marc Rosenberg, "The Coming Knowledge Tsunami."

at mid-career are rethinking what *our future of work* looks like because we are doing things that are vastly different from what we had expected to do and we see how the world has evolved, then we **cannot** ignore what this means for future generations.

PART I:

DEVELOPING THE SELF

Aristotle said that *"Knowing yourself is the beginning of all wisdom."*

Unfortunately, nowadays, some young people mistake self-awareness to be the navel gazing displayed by influencers on social media, or celebrities because of their brand building, but they need to be taught that simply having a brand is not self-awareness. There are so many lifestyle gurus, all over the web, especially on Instagram. These influencers are shilling products, or workouts, or courses. But ultimately, they are shilling a lifestyle to the teens and young adults of today; a life in which they too can be in the blissful turquoise water, or in a poolside cabana looking like they stepped out of the pages of *Vogue*, or poised in a tree pose on top of a mountain looking at a glorious sunrise. This is savvy marketing. But just as the ads of yesteryear tried to convince everyone that a product, any product, was the revolutionary thing that would transform a person's reality into a picture-perfect life, life does not change with the purchase of that product, brand, or service. Real change within one's life comes from knowing oneself.

It is daunting to consider how much work goes into developing one's self and helping young people, children, and young adults, develop these skills, but we must keep the long view in mind. The children of today are the adults of tomorrow. Though, they do not know how to or need to delve so deeply into developing the *self*, we need to begin their development of these skills. Once these young people are past the most sheltered part of their lives—childhood, and head into adulthood—they will be managing the pressures that are unique to being an adult. Navigating from childhood into adulthood, they will develop deeper more meaningful relationships and friendships. They will begin to deal with the pressures of a workplace. Stress factors change over time because as one ages, the responsibilities in life change. Self-management skills are vital for dealing with external influences.

Emotional intelligence, resilience, adaptability, critical thinking, and complex problem-solving are key skills for the *future of work* because the world is more interconnected than before. In the Fourth Industrial Revolution routine and basic tasks of jobs will be lost to automation and the skills that are uniquely human are what will survive.

If there's an advantage you want to give your child or children, developing the *self* is the place to start.

CHAPTER 2:

EMOTIONAL INTELLIGENCE

———

In a recent training I conducted, where the participants were young millennials and gen-z, one of the participants raised the question that, if their generations were able to label and understand the emotion, why didn't it make them more emotionally intelligent? Why are there so many more *"trigger"* warnings now than there used to be? As I reflected on his words, I thought about how the millennial and gen-z generations are better at labeling their emotions compared to previous generations. I answered that being able to label and understand emotions does not constitute learning how to cope with them. Knowing the emotions is a start but being able to manage the emotions is what is needed, and that management comes through the skill of emotional intelligence.

As parents, teachers, leaders of our society, we have helped the younger generations with the *"capacity to recognize their own feelings"* and maybe to some extent recognize the feelings in others, but we have not taken the next step of teaching them how to cope with and manage their feelings and the feelings of others.

Any *future of work* or skills gap report that is published today, includes emotional intelligence (EI) as a top soft skill that is essential for the workplace. The world economic forum's *Future of Jobs* report from 2018, ranks emotional intelligence as number eight in the growing skills needed for the workforce of 2022. With, 2022 being around the corner, and the rapid acceleration of artificial intelligence in the workplace, as we stand poised at the starting edge of the Fourth Industrial Revolution, our human skills are relevant and necessary now more than ever.

Daniel Goleman, the pioneer of emotional intelligence, defines emotional intelligence as *"the capacity to recognize our own feelings and those of others, and to manage emotions effectively in ourselves and our relationships."*[20] In this chapter, I focus on the foundation of emotional intelligence, which is recognizing, understanding, and managing the emotions of one's self. As I shared with the participants in my training, recognition and knowledge of emotions have improved compared to the past, but they still have a long way to go and must be accompanied by management of emotions.

SELF-AWARENESS

During each of the interviews I conducted as part of my research for this book, the first skill each interviewee said that the youth will need to succeed in the workplace is

20 Daniel Goleman, *Working with Emotional Intelligence.* (317).

self-awareness. It is no wonder that self-awareness is the cornerstone of emotional intelligence because without knowing one's self, how can we expect others to know us.

"Everything starts with self-awareness."

WARREN WRIGHT, CEO SECOND WAVE LEARNING

Self-awareness is a key competency in all spheres of life. The business leaders I interviewed, emphasized this competency because they see it missing or underdeveloped in young professionals today. Because of this missing competency, these leaders feel that young people are not equipped to handle the many demands of the workplace because of all the different people and stakeholders that they must interact with. The leaders feel that a lack of self-awareness is what leads to inadequate self-management of emotions and reactions, and to poor self-management in dealing with the uncertainties of life. And heading into the future of work, the people who will be most successful in finding and retaining employment will be the ones that can optimize their human skills because jobs that can be automated, or jobs that can be augmented with artificial intelligence will be taken away from people. But until human emotions, experience, understanding of nuances and contexts–these unique human traits can be replicated by machines, it is these characteristics that give us the advantage in gaining employment and being employed.

The journey to self-awareness begins by pausing and reflecting over what we feel, when we feel it, and why we feel it. The process of figuring this out can be discomforting because it requires time to think about the emotions and we seem to live in a world of distractions. Yes, in this day and age it seems we have more options to distract ourselves than in the past, but it's not a new practice. Distractions take us away from the discomfort, which is what we need to *lean into* to improve this skill. In identifying what triggers our emotional and physical responses, we can work toward managing them. For instance, one of the people I interviewed, shared anonymously that the reason she began smoking in college was because when she would wait for her friends to meet her someplace, it gave her something to do. She especially relied on smoking when she would be waiting at bars or restaurants for people to meet up with her, back in the day when smoking indoors was still allowed. She wasn't comfortable being by herself with nothing to do. In her opinion the phone addiction stems from the same feeling of being uncomfortable with just sitting with one's thoughts.

As a parent of two boys, I have noticed a larger social trend which allows for boys to express and verbalize their feelings and accept that it's okay to feel emotional. A huge improvement from the previous generations where to be a *"man"* meant no crying or showing emotion. But regardless of gender, understanding and expressing emotions should be common practice with young children. Young kids don't have as many challenges, obstacles, or stressors compared to adults. They also tend to have a support system of adults that are around them such as parents, coaches, families, teachers, and others. Therefore, if we begin the journey of self-awareness skills from a young age, we are helping them build emotional intelligence as a habit.

Self-awareness is the foundation because when kids have strong self-awareness skills, they[21]:

- know their strengths and areas to improve
- can organize and prioritize things in their life to complete a task
- are able to see mistakes in their work, and correct them
- understand and can discuss their feelings
- identify the emotions and needs of other people
- can see how their behavior impacts others
- develop a growth mindset
- become more resilient and can see and learn from their mistakes

Being self-aware builds self-esteem and gives children the courage to speak up for what they need. Self-awareness will serve them in being authentic and strong as they age. As kids enter their middle school and high school years, followed by their college years, they begin to face challenges in friendships and relationships. More stressors begin to get added into their lives. But by being self-aware, they are able to navigate the challenges of growing up with a lot more confidence.

Self-awareness is understanding yourself at a very honest and intimate level. Knowing the actions that you're taking, the feelings that you are feeling, and where your blind spots exist; that is self-awareness. Your actions and feelings, when you face an unfamiliar context, or when you have to juggle multiple obligations, or how you deal with different personalities

---

21   Amanda Morin, "The Importance of Self-Awareness in Kids."

are all being self-aware. Knowing how you react when all these things collide is self-awareness. It is also knowing your strengths and weaknesses.

And, since we don't live in a vacuum, it is also about knowing how our traits present or emerge in situations to those around us. Naturally, some of our traits are more appealing to those around us whereas other traits are not. So, another aspect of self-awareness is about knowing how others perceive us. When kids are self-aware, they understand that how they see themselves may be different from how others see them. As adults we can help our youth cultivate the traits that are positive and give them feedback on how to manage those negative tendencies; to be forgiving of the negative in themselves and others. No one is perfect, so flaws exist; but it's how you respond when the negative comes out that matters.

Our goal is to teach our youth, that the path to self-awareness is to do the hard work of developing self-awareness. That we must do the deep work of knowing our emotions, knowing our strengths and weaknesses as we know them, as others know them, and to do this requires introspection. After knowing all this, comes the next step, which is management of those emotions because awareness of self on its own is not enough.

SELF-MANAGEMENT

Several memes out there are on how millennials are *"snowflakes"* and demand rewards, need recognition for every little thing they do, and that they are incapable of handling the demands of the real world. That's because in the past, management of emotions could be summed up with seven words *"suck it up and deal with it."* While, there may be an element of truth in the desire for recognition and rewards being greater in younger generations, what older generations fail to acknowledge is that if young people are unable to deal with life, it's because the adults have not prepared them. And that old method for managing emotions or impulses—*"developing a thick skin"*—well that hasn't worked out so well. The world is a vastly divided place economically, socially, or politically, and these divisions have always existed, but the gap between the two ends is increasing. Without self-management or coping skills, the basis of resilience, we're going to find that much like the younger generations in the workforce today, the youth of now will continue to experience the *"deer in headlights"* type of reactions.

We don't live in vacuums. We have to deal with people around us. But before we manage our relationships with others, we need to be able to manage our own selves. We need to be able to manage our actions and reactions in response to our emotions. Our capacity to show emotional intelligence through emotional self-management will vary at times depending on the intensity of the demands that we experience. So, at times we won't have to put more than the usual effort of coping, but there are times where things are a lot more turbulent, and we will have to put more effort into managing our emotions. We haven't prepared the current generations, millennials and gen-z, to manage their emotions in that turbulent state of being. We're not preparing future generations either because we have tried to shield our youth from the different things that they're going to be facing in the real world.

One tool that was developed to help individuals regulate their emotional self-control and manage post-traumatic stress is *"trigger warnings."* Trigger warnings, started in academia and then started seeping into other facets of our environment, such as work, personal life, or relationships. The Australian Psychological Society writes that *"the idea of trigger warnings originates in the psychiatric literature on post-traumatic reactions, because the primary features of post-traumatic stress disorder (PTSD) include 're-experiencing symptoms,' like intrusive thoughts and flashbacks."*[22] *Such thoughts tend to occur involuntarily because like the word trigger is defined, the action does not occur in a general sense but rather it is mechanic and automatic, like a reflex. Unfortunately, over time the term "triggered" or trigger warning has become* a very broad and loose term that encompasses warnings against not just things that are traumatic but also to things that are offensive, political, or anything that is contrary to an individual's point of view. Regrettably, what is beginning to happen is that the tool has become a protection against developing the self-awareness and self-management skills that are needed to live through life.

When such tools are present, it's important to prevent them from being usurped to achieve the opposite of why they exist. Self-awareness teaches us why we feel what we feel, and self-management helps us figure out how to harness or direct those emotions or reactions. We cannot go through life without feeling discomfort and we need to model that for our youth because even though avoidance to manage uneasiness

---

22 Nick Haslam, "What's the Difference Between Traumatic Fear and Moral Anger? Trigger Warnings Won't Tell You."

is not a new technique, with technology we can be instantly distracted and do not have to be unsettled at all. Growth comes from change and change comes from being challenged or being forced to face or try new things. Self-management is a power struggle within ourselves–between choosing what is easy in the short run and bad long-term vs. what is hard in the short-term but better in the long run. Unfortunately, humans tend to pick the things that are easy or provide immediate gratification. Another thing we need to remember is that though we possess a mix of negative and positive traits, it doesn't mean we're either inherently good or bad. Similarly, emotions are neither good nor bad, and emotions cannot be turned on and off with a switch. Instead of the old methods of trying to *"toughen"* up our kids we need to help them *"deal"* with it by teaching and modeling the techniques to emotionally manage ourselves. Because self-awareness may be the foundational skill of EI, without self-management the awareness only gets a person so far.

Besides emotions, there is another aspect of self-management by which adults are often judged. That is a person's capability to handle their life and their work. The so-called world of adulting. Adults are expected to have a job, work, and keep up with their professional deadlines and obligations. Additionally, adults should also be able to pay their bills on time, manage their finances, cook for themselves, clean and house keep, have a means for transportation, get married, and have a family. These are the markers of adulthood as set forth by society and being able to stay on top of these things or be working toward these long-term goals are what people are judged on. Self-sufficiency is considered to be a successful demonstration of self-management skills and some of the social goals listed require practical skills of cooking and knowing how to budget, and so on. However, by far the largest part of our lives have to do with us and our relationships with others. So, by focusing on the higher order skills that develop our youth's emotional intelligence or problem-solving skills, we're equipping them with the foundations to be self-sufficient in both their professional and personal lives.

DEVELOPING EMOTIONAL INTELLIGENCE

IDENTIFY EMOTIONS

First, we need to help identify the emotions that youth (and we all) experience. The whole range of them from positive to negative because we want them to be able to identify them as such. Keep in mind that negative emotion simply means that it causes stress or is mentally harmful if it is unchecked. Emotions aren't inherently good or bad. As mentioned in my training experience above, I feel that we have done a good job of labeling emotions, and we should keep that going.

- Surround kids with books about emotions. As a parent or an educator, having these books around for you to read to them or for them to read is very important.
- Emojis are also a great tool to use to identify emotions. For tweens and teens, emojis can be a low stress way of identifying emotions. Teachers, these are a great way to gauge your students' emotions across all ages.
- Parents talk about your own emotions. If you haven't engaged in such conversations with them so far, model

it for them and talk about your emotions. Start with positive and add in the negative.

IDENTIFY TRIGGERS

Strong emotions are often accompanied by physical symptoms, and physical symptoms are easier to identify than powerful emotions at times. It requires a lot of self-awareness to connect the physical to the emotional, and so by making that connection for them we're helping them figure out the triggers for the strong emotions, and how to handle those feelings.

- When you see them exhibiting a strong emotion, talk them through it at that time. Ask them questions about how they physically feel. With very young children, give them the vocabulary they need to express themselves. With older children, let them respond on their own. Ask them questions about physical feelings, like what are they physically feeling? Is there pain anywhere? Do they feel any tingling? Are they breathing faster or slower? What about the expression on their face? Does their body feel light, Or does it feel heavy? Ask questions that are appropriate to the emotion they are exhibiting.
- Encourage them to journal. Have them think about, reflect on their day, their emotions. As part of disciplining children, encourage them to examine how their emotions impact their actions. Encourage them to write about why they might have felt what they did. It may not be authentic at first, but it starts building that self-awareness. Tie it into a routine for them at bedtime, or after school.

- In dealing with older children, especially teenagers, be calm whenever you talk to them. Don't let your judgments come through. Also, don't overdo the conversation if they're not in the mood. Remain persistent though because teenagers need to be able to manage their emotions, and help them identify physical symptoms.

MANAGE EMOTIONS

The world does not see the hard work on the self; what they see is the result—how well we can manage ourselves emotionally. They want to see how one reacts under times of stress or when things change at the last minute whether the person is proactive and in control as opposed to being reactive to what is around.

- Model how you manage your emotions, both positive and negative, and depending on the age group of the child, model at the appropriate level.
- Parents—create your own decompression ritual. Take time to meditate or do deep breathing or reflect and invite them to join you. At least announce that you're taking the time to do this and encourage them to come and join you. If you're stuck at a traffic light, find pockets of time to show them that mindfulness is ongoing.
- Teachers—create a *"calm"* corner or an *"I need a moment"* corner in your classroom. For older students, or when students move through the classrooms, teachers take a moment to explain what students can do if they need a moment. Can they stand quietly at the back of the class? Can they put their head down for a few minutes? Think

of ways or brainstorm with your students how they would like to take the time to emotionally calm down.

Most importantly, remember that telling them doesn't always work. Show them, invite them, and encourage them to build these habits by illustrating the way that you build and maintain your emotional self-awareness and emotional self-management. Separate how intrinsically linked is a part of self-management that is taking responsibility for our being and our actions and how we conduct ourselves in the world, personally or professionally.

CHAPTER 3:

RESILIENCE

————

Imagine being hired as training lead for a massive global training deployment. You arrive at the kickoff meeting, and you're in front of the stakeholders ready to launch this project. You're full of energy and excited to have this opportunity. You are proud of your hard work and just feeling good about yourself. Your boss steps up and introduces you to the crowd of forty or so people in front of you–the people you're there to help navigate through these new upgrades. And in walks a leader from another department and announces that a member of their department is the training lead. There you are in front of all the key people to help make this project a success, and you have been undermined in front of them. How would you feel?

Stunned? Upset? Flabbergasted? All the above!

This is what happened to Sonia Baker[23], a lead trainer for several prominent companies over the past quarter of a century plus.

————

23   Name has been changed at interviewee's request.

Fortunately for Ms. Baker, her boss immediately stepped in to clear up the confusion and quickly informed the other person and the department that Sonia was the training lead, and so the kickoff proceeded. While Sonia was lucky to have such a supportive boss, she was also left to work with a person who thought that they were going to be leading the project but were not. It was a two-year long project that got off to a very rocky start. The woman, who was passed over, expressed her disappointment openly at work and at times in a rather unprofessional manner. This made it difficult to do the work but Sonia credits her resilience to be able to move past the challenging start and find ways to work with her colleague, even when she, Sonia, had to bear the brunt of her colleague's outbursts.

In a survey conducted by two British researchers, they found that 75 percent of the employees said that the biggest drain on their resilience was dealing with difficult people at work or office politics.[24] And of the nearly thirty interviews that I conducted, one of the chief complaints by business leaders was the lack of resilience in their young employees. In fact, after self-awareness, resilience was the most desired soft skill because resilience is the ability to bounce back after a setback. Life is a rollercoaster, full of successes and setbacks.

Psychologists define resilience as *"the process of adapting well in the face of adversity, trauma, tragedy, threats or significant sources of stress."*[25] Resilience is closely linked to knowing yourself and is an aspect of managing yourself. Parents tend

---

24   Andrea Ovans, "What Resilience Means, and Why It Matters."

25   Palmiter, et al., "Building Your Resilience."

to shield their children from adversity or stressful experiences. And when children are young, they don't have to deal with the stressors of family, friends, work, health, or finances, so the need for developing resilience is not as strong.

But as children grow older, the course of life is such that they begin to experience the stresses of managing relationships with family and friends, and managing school work. Parents help them manage those. Some parents take it to an extreme. We're all familiar with the term *"helicopter parents."* Parents that hover and micromanage and overprotect their children to an extreme. In the past couple of years, a new term has emerged for a more extreme version of parenting *"snowplow parents."* Like a snowplow, these parents remove any obstacle in the way of their children.[26] An excellent example of such parents would be the celebrities involved in the college admissions scandal who took whatever measures they could to ensure that their children could get whatever they wanted without any difficulty or disappointment.

Parents who over-parent, through helicopter parenting, snowplow parenting, or any kind of parenting style that focuses on micromanaging everything for their children, think that by removing obstacles, they are creating a direct path to success. In reality, they are doing the exact opposite. Without learning how to deal with smaller adversities, how will these children grow into adulthood and handle the pressures that come with it? The setbacks they experience as adults will be bigger and have greater consequences. We

---

26 Emma Waverman, "Snowplow Parenting: What to Know About the Controversial Technique."

need to teach them to be able to bounce back after failures because life is not without disappointments. As parents we should be supporting our kids through failure more than preventing it. We should be teaching them how to recover from setbacks. It's natural to want to protect our children, to shelter them, and maybe there are times that are appropriate to do that. However, we also need to let them fail. It may be uncomfortable, but never forget that we are raising children to be the adults they will be, and we want them to be resilient.

As old norms shift, we will all need to embrace lifelong learning to grow and succeed in our jobs. The *"learn-unlearn-re-learn"* cycle we will need to engage in during the *future of work* requires resilience. Learning is a growth process and some things will be easier to learn while others won't. Whether we learn it the first go around or it takes us ten more times, it doesn't matter. What does matter is that if we don't learn it the first go around, we try again. We keep trying and we ask for help. Such behavior requires resilience.

In Daniel Goleman's Emotional and Social Intelligence Leadership Competency Model, of the twelve competencies in the four domains of emotional intelligence, there are two competencies that he states are the basis for resiliency, and those competencies are positive outlook and achievement orientation.[27]

In the late twentieth century and early twenty-first century a *"Successory"* poster was the epitome of office decor. If you

---

27   "Emotional and Social Intelligence Leadership Competencies: An Overview."

were important enough to have an office, you had one of those posters on your wall. The poster would have a motivational word or phrase like *"Integrity"* or *"Believe & Succeed"* along with a brief platitude under this bold heading. Both these were at the bottom of a natural backdrop–something that would evoke that word–like the teamwork *"Successory"* poster has a pack of wolves as the picture. These posters were a statement. A statement of a value or a trait important to either the person displaying it, the company, or both. But they were also meant to be uplifting and inspiring along with being motivating and positive.

Plenty of research indicates that having a positive outlook leads to a longer and healthier life. Positive outlook is the ability to see the positives in people, situations, and events, even those that on the surface seem less than positive. To develop a positive outlook extends beyond just telling a person to *"be positive"* because our brains are wired to focus more on the negative than the positive; knowing and filtering the negative kept us out of harm's way evolutionarily. As noted in the magazine, *Psychology Today*, positive and negative interactions don't balance out in a fifty-fifty manner because of the brain's predisposition toward holding onto negative emotions and information, so to counteract the negative there should be a ratio of five positive acts or emotions to one negative.[28] In practice, positive outlook is looking at failures or setbacks as growth opportunities, and looking toward the future with a positive attitude that there is the potential for good things to come, and to perceive people in a positive light by focusing on positive traits and interactions.

---

28   Hara Marano, "Our Brain's Negative Bias."

Achievement orientation is the competency of trying to meet and exceed high standards, taking in feedback, then striving to improve and do better. Goleman says that in professional circumstances, achievement orientation is an individual's competency that has to be balanced with the needs of the organization. Individuals who are strong in the achievement orientation competency tend to do really well in their personal achievement of taking on new positions and growing in their career, which is an important quality to have in charting non-linear career paths.[29]

I know as a mother I battle with my kids over the amount of time they want to spend playing video games. However, video games are a great example of achievement orientation. While completing a game, the player has to go through many levels, staying focused on the objective of defeating the boss, rescuing the princess, or whatever the final objective is. If you've ever watched someone playing a video game, you can see the intensity in trying to beat or win the level. The player is passionate, motivated, and focused. The player will keep trying new ways to try to defeat a level, take risks by experimenting with new tools or tactics. This illustrates achievement orientation perfectly because often, the game defeats the player and the player must persist to reach the goal. Failures are a natural part of it, but the passion and motivation keep the player going. Now this doesn't mean I give carte blanche to my kids about video games, but I do remind myself of the benefits that can come from it.

---

29   Daniel Goleman, "Balance Your Need to Achieve."

"The difference between winners and losers is how they handle losing."

ROSABETH MOSS KANTER, PROFESSOR

HARVARD BUSINESS SCHOOL[30]

People who handle losing with grace—they acknowledge their disappointment but take the loss as an opportunity to improve for the next time—are resilient. Resilience does not mean that there isn't room for disappointment, frustration, or anger. As I wrote in the previous chapter, emotions aren't good or bad, but how we respond or react to them is what leads to good or bad behavior.

During the summer of 2019, my nephew, Hassen who had completed his junior year at college traveled to Prague, Czech Republic's, Anglo American University for a study-abroad course. Virginia Commonwealth University, from where Hassen will graduate with a dual degree in Political Science and Business in May 2020, offers an international consulting program where over four weeks, students can complete two classes and earn six credits. The classes, Principles of Consulting I and II, gave students an opportunity to work with other study-abroad students on specific consulting deliverables for local companies. For the first course, he spent two weeks working with students from Mexico on market analysis for a feedback agency in Richmond. And for the next two weeks, he worked with students in Prague on a project

---

30 Rosabeth Kanter, "Surprises Are the New Normal; Resilience Is the New Skill."

for UNICEF CZ–the Czech Republic's office. He was part of a group that helped UNICEF CZ with optimizing their Facebook page. They learned about Facebook's algorithm, social media content, market analysis, and other metrics to accomplish their deliverable.

Hassen had decided to spend a couple of weeks after his class ended traveling in Europe. It wasn't his first time abroad; in fact, he has been privileged enough to have visited all seven continents. So, he was familiar with how much travel demands of one, yet he still found himself struggling at times because this was his first time traveling alone extensively. Hassen is one of four, and is outgoing, charming, and lively but being alone is not his strong suit. He also didn't go in with a very firm plan because he didn't want to feel *"disappointed for not completing his itinerary"* in case he didn't do all that he had planned. Turns out, having a plan of some sort helps. Hassen shared with me some of the mental and emotional struggle of not having someone to help you with decision making, to split up responsibilities with, or just sharing the experience with someone, but he feels that he learned a lot about himself. He has lots of lessons learned should he be in such a situation again, but what kept him going was that grit. He recognized that he had an opportunity to grow and learn. He found ways to manage the situation, including asking people for help, researching online, and discovering *"more travel blogs"* than he had *"expected to ever find."* Even though he could have given up and gone home, an option that was available to him, he was resilient enough to work through the challenges.

Setbacks and failures are a natural part of life. Some of them occur because of our own errors, and others occur because of circumstances that are outside our control. Those with low resilience can be broken and may never recover. Whereas those with a strong sense of resilience are able to pick up the pieces and move on. In a rapidly changing world and work environment, people who have the ability to fail fast and get back to trying afterward will be able to adapt and succeed, a key reason why resilience is an important skill to develop.

Think about the last time you experienced widespread change in your workplace. Whether it's company-wide, or just your department and your team. Most likely people's reactions could be divided into two responses. The first response is most likely to be one of *"Why do we keep changing things that work just fine? All it does is create more problems."* The second response is probably along the lines of *"This sucks, but I guess it will be worth it in the long run."* Both responses acknowledge the frustrations of changing, and of unlearning old systems and learning new ones. However, the first response comes from a place of resistance, and with that resistance will come stress. With extra stress there will be burnout. The second response comes from a place of understanding the tradeoff between short-term pain for long-term success. There will be stress but it's a more positive outlook, so, the toll is not as significant compared to what the person with the first type of response will experience. There are more than only these two responses, but these exemplify the spectrum.

Reframing the narrative to a more positive outlook—people who take the longer view or see the benefits even if the benefits aren't immediate, they demonstrate a higher level of resilience. Individuals who can see the long-term benefits for short-term sacrifices will find it easier to embrace life-long learning. Because of the current skills gap, our workforce is already behind in being ready for the new era of work. Who are the people that you want to work with? Do you want to work with people who will fight or complain every time a change takes place? Do you want to work with people who will handle it and find the path forward? I'm a mother of a tween and a teen and they could be entering the workforce as soon as the next five or six years unless they go to college to earn a bachelor's first; in the next ten to twelve years. I want them to be the kind of coworker that has the second response to change. The kind of person who won't take negative feedback and stew over it, or as in the case of Sonia's colleague, a person who experienced a tough loss, decided to respond to it by taking her anger out on other people or yelling and throwing tantrums. I want them to see setbacks and failures with the lens of growth opportunities.

The World Economic Forum has put in place a platform for the "Re-skilling Revolution" to help people prepare for the new opportunities that will be open to them.[31] Resilience itself is a skill in the skills gap but is also needed to close those skills gaps. We cannot let our kids grow up without developing this very important skill, because we will all need to have that grit. That curiosity to give us the strength and courage to keep learning, growing, and charting out a career in this new world of work.

---

31   "Reskilling Revolution Program."

BUILDING RESILIENCE

Helping our kids develop resilience will help them in their winding career paths and life paths because with resilience they will be able to deal with the adversity that they're going to experience in trying to navigate their way through the new way of life and work in the Fourth Industrial Revolution. Not to mention that this is a key skill in making our way through the ups and downs of life.

- Optimism is a key aspect of resilience. Teaching our children to look at the bright side or to think in more positive terms is a way to help them build this key skill. Helping them look at things more optimistically is the first step, but this is one of those skills that requires a lot of modeling because they need to hear it, see it, and deeply ingrain it because our brains tend to hold on to negatives longer than positives.
- Adult relationships, those outside of parents, also have a lasting effect on resilience. Having positive influences like teachers, coaches, grandparents, friends, or family members also help because children have another adult to turn to when they are facing adversity or toughness of any sort. Parents–help them foster such relationships with trusted members of your community. Teachers–never underestimate your powers.
- Allow children to experience failures and face natural consequences. Don't rescue them when they forget something they're supposed to do. If they miss out on family responsibilities, then have reminders which lead to natural consequences. Same with academic and other personal responsibilities. Consistency is key.

- Provide opportunities to build on successes and to take on large responsibilities. Kids who know that they're good at something and who have healthy self-esteem are more resilient because they have a sense of identity. They don't lose their sense of self when there is a crisis. By taking on responsibilities and being able to handle those successfully, their self-esteem increases and builds resilience. However, remember not to step in if they struggle.
- Learning how to manage stress is another important facet of building resilience. Schoolwork, friendships, and family relationships can all induce stress in children, but they need to learn how to manage it. So, from an early age encourage mindfulness. Have them be aware of the physical, emotional, and mental manifestations of stress. Lead them in meditation, yoga, exercise, or journaling to help them reduce the stress. Instill in them the idea of what is within their control and what is not. Help them think through what they can do about the things that are in their control and how to handle those things that are not.
- Travel brings many opportunities to develop resilience, and it doesn't have to be solo travel. Parents–take your kids on trips whether domestic or international. Between long journeys, itineraries to keep, and being in an unfamiliar environment, there are opportunities for children to work on their resilience with the love and help of a parent. Depending on their age, they can also be responsible from packing for their travel to planning part of the itinerary.

We can't shelter our kids from the hard things in life, but we can give them the tools to prevent the hard things from derailing them.

CHAPTER 4:

ADAPTABILITY

———

In 2015, Ayesha Sethi, current Founder of Sethi Learning & Company in Karachi, Pakistan, embarked on a solo adventure. She was headed to Gaziantep, a city in Southern Turkey to teach English to students at Gaziantep University. It was her first time traveling outside of Pakistan on her own, and to a destination that was completely unknown and where she had no support network of any sort. Ms. Sethi had volunteered for this experience because she wanted to challenge herself and *"increase her appetite for risk."* She soon got more than she had bargained for. It was the first time where she felt that the experience *"tested my agility to an extreme because I was well beyond my comfort zone."* In Gaziantep, she found that few—less than one percent of the population—spoke any of the languages she knew including English.

She had no one to turn to for help—no safety net. Even if she had had an emergency, communicating with the authorities would have been hard because of the language barrier. Basic tasks like commuting to work or purchasing groceries were a struggle because of the language impediment, and she was alone in trying to figure all of this out.

"Suddenly survival felt like a privilege."

Fortunately, with the help of apps and by learning basic Turkish, she was able to navigate her way through the experience overall, but the learning curve was steep. One where she found her *"cognitive flexibility tested"* all the time. Using her resilience, she made a conscious effort to open herself to experience, to learn local customs for social acceptance, and conduct herself according to the norms of the place. She found that *"agility becomes all the more difficult when you are the only one in that boat."* However, her only option was to adapt because she had volunteered for this and committed for a six-week course.

From her experience, Ayesha learned the importance of making an effort to push one's self out of one's regular routines so that brain muscles are stretched. We all need to have the mental flexibility to juggle tasks, uncertainty, and new events that zoom into our lives out of nowhere. And without being adaptable, that is difficult to achieve in practice. *"Our orderly routines continue to propel us more and more toward a fixed mindset,"* says Ms. Sethi, and I agree completely. Her advice, *"staying agile requires awareness of not only its importance but also a deliberate effort to challenge our boundaries on a regular basis."*

Adaptability is defined as the ability to change or adjust yourself to a new situation or environment or to reach a goal. It doesn't mean that you become a different person or change your goals; it means that you find ways to acclimate to the change. Some people use adaptability and flexibility synonymously. A flexible person is often thought to be adaptable, but

I would like to make a distinction between these two terms. Flexibility is more of a short-term trait–in the moment– whereas adaptability is the capacity to sustain long-term change. Being adaptable allows for a person to change and adjust their solutions, techniques, or jobs as needed in the new context. Being flexible allows a person to adjust to a specific situation, or to be okay with someone else making a decision that also impacts you. Adaptability is not losing track of your goals or changing focus but having the skills to reach your goal in a different way than planned because we recognize that life throws us a lot of different things. For today's youth the pace of such changes in the workplace will be more rapid and accelerated. So, developing adaptability as a skill in our youth is critical, especially as some of those significant changes are already underway.

Nearly twenty years ago, at the start of the century, the Agile software development process was created because the processes that existed at that time for software development, were following older engineering practices, and in the 1990s, with the technology boom, businesses were moving at a much more rapid pace, and software development was lagging because the developers couldn't get the technology to its users quickly enough.[32] In 2000, leaders in the software development met and articulated the need for adaptability during the process, and in 2001 the Agile Manifesto was created as a means to discover better ways of developing software.[33] Though it's been almost two decades since the

---

32 Peter Varhol, "To Agility and Beyond: The History—and Legacy—of Agile Development."

33 Beck, et al., "Manifesto for Agile Software Development."

manifesto and origin of Agile, it has taken over a decade for the process to become popular to the point of being ubiquitous. Moreover, nowadays other business processes are using agile or similar methods to try to stay nimble and flexible. It is important to note here that the need for adaptability arose due to changing consumer expectations and demands, but it took almost ten years to come up with a method that allowed for the flexibility and adaptability needed. In the past, ten years was too slow; in the future ten minutes might be too slow.

Today's youth is going to face so many unknowns like climate change, jobs, living situations, and add to it that there are going to be other challenges that we can't even imagine and the impact that all this will have on their lives. We already live in a volatile, uncertain, complex, and ambiguous (VUCA) world. And if you look at the new trends and new avenues of how we work in the modern workplace, trends like open office spaces, co-working spaces, food and games, nap rooms, along with tackling issues like gender diversity, mental health, pay equity, work-life integration, plus new ways to work like remote or telework, participating in the gig economy, artificial intelligence, and robot integration. There's a lot that is going on in the workplace and will be even more in the future.

More and more people are rejecting the idea of traditional nine to five employment. More opportunities are found as part of the gig economy—people working for themselves and charting their own path as freelancers, contractors, or participating in the sharing economy. The development of new work opportunities like ride sharing or renting out rooms and homes has made it easier for people to participate in the gig economy. Companies like Uber, Lyft, Instacart, Byrd, and Airbnb have allowed people to enter the gig workforce with relative ease and to cobble together employment equivalent to that of a full-time job or beyond because a *"gig"* is temporary work, and the worker is paid only for that specific job.

"The gig economy is not new–people have always worked gigs... but today when most people refer to the "gig economy," they're specifically talking about new technology-enabled kinds of work."[34]

MOLLY TURNER, DIRECTOR (FORMER)

PUBLIC POLICY, AIRBNB

Some people are part of the gig economy as a side hustle, like Maher a college student at George Mason University, who delivers food for Doordash, and Rachel, a mother of elementary aged kids, who works for Instacart and Lyft to bring in additional income during the hours her kids are at school. Others who retired from jobs do ride-sharing services full-time to help supplement their retirement income. In the Washington DC area and its surroundings, many ride-sharing drivers are recent immigrants who support their families through driving for such services. Recently, one of the Lyft

34 Emilia Istrate and Jonathan Harris, "The Future of Work: The Rise of the Gig Economy."

drivers that I met during my use of the service, Emile, was a recent graduate who sold seasonal merchandise online, traded cryptocurrency, and drove for Lyft. He started his online business while still in college, and it generated enough revenue that he continued to add in more *"gig"* type work to maintain his independence over his working hours. He knew he wouldn't do this forever but for the time being it allowed him the opportunity to work when he wanted, and to learn about new things that interested him along the way.

Emile is not alone in carving out an employment path in the gig economy. In fact, many recent graduates participate in different facets of the gig economy. In a 2019 *Forbes* article, contributor Abdullahi Muhammed, advises new graduates to be prepared to create their own employment path because many of them will not be able to secure a job as soon as they graduate. And while that may seem daunting, it can in fact be a very good thing.[35] Muhammed writes that, *"Forty percent of gig workers net over six-figures per year and the majority didn't spend a decade climbing the career ladder to secure such paychecks."*[36] So even though there may not be the stability of traditional employment, those who have skills that are in demand can create their own path, a path that can put them ahead in the long run as compared to the traditional employment route. In fact, Muhammed further states that *"Forty percent of companies state that gig workers will become a major part of their workforce within several years. What's*

---

35   Abdullahi Muhammed, "Busting the Gig Economy Myths: 40% of Gig Workers Now Earn Six-Figures Per Year."

36   Ibid.

even more important is that they are ready to offer top com-
pensation to the skilled contractors."[37]

Working for multiple employers and keeping track of responsibilities requires strong adaptability skills. It may seem like a
small thing, but in ridesharing for instance, you must adapt
to your passenger or customer's needs. Some passengers prefer to ride in silence, while others like to chat. Then there is
pool ridesharing in which you're serving multiple customers
at the same time. On the other hand, if you're also working
as a personal shopper, that requires a different set of skills
such as reaching out and connecting with the customers to
provide them different options in case the primary option
is missing. Faith Popcorn, a futurist, says that we will all
have to become as agile as possible and *"have many forms
of talent and work that you can provide the economy...and
in the future we'll all have seven or eight jobs, with the average adult working for a number of companies simultaneously
rather than working for one big corporation."*[38]

The skill of adaptability in self and adaptability in life—to
be able to assess the context and be able to figure out how
to mold yourself, if needed, to adapt to that context is a key
competency. The clearest example of contextual adaptability
is in our daily interactions—how we act differently with our
co-workers versus our friends versus our family. Our verbal
and nonverbal communication is different in each of these
contexts. Moreover, even within our relationship groups, we

---

37 Ibid.

38 Arwa Mahdawi, "What Jobs Will Still Be Around in 20 Years? Read This
to Prepare Your Future."

may be more accommodating to some people over others like our parents, siblings, or children. The nature of the relationship does impact our contextual adaptability; however, it is all part of the same aspect. Another type of contextual ability is when we have to take a different route due to road closures, or if there's an item missing from a recipe and we substitute a different item for it. These are all small changes that we find ourselves handling and adapting to routinely, and because of its routine, there tends to be less resistance to it. Inconvenience and grumbling relate to that, but there isn't a deep-rooted resistance.

Diane Mulcahy, author of *The Gig Economy: The Complete Guide to Getting Better Work, Taking More Time Off, and Financing the Life you Want*, writes in an October 2019 *Harvard Business Review* article that universities should be preparing students for the gig economy.[39] Nearly 20 to 30 percent of the United States' working-age population participate in some type of independent or *"gig"* type of work.[40] In fact, the majority of Google's workforce comprises independent and temporary workers rather than full-time employees.[41] Mulcahy recommends that universities should take the following steps to help students get ready for being a part of the gig economy.

---

39   Diane Mulcahy, "Universities Should Be Preparing Students for the Gig Economy."

40   Manyika, et al., "Independent Work: Choice, Necessity, and the Gig Economy."

41   Daisuke Wakabayashi, "Google's Shadow Work Force: Temps Who Outnumber Full-Time Employees."

1. First, teach students basic skills to work independently—the basics of managing a business, contracts, accounting, and so forth.
2. Second, expand career services to include gig opportunities and encourage students to take part in independent or project work opportunities even while they're in college.
3. Third, practice what they preach since many universities are staffed with independent contractors–adjunct professors.

In addition to the increased number of gig workers, remote work trends have also risen rapidly in the past decade where now at least 70 percent of professionals work remotely from home at least once, and as of 2018, 4.3 million Americans work from home, making up 3.2 percent of the workforce. Nearly half, 47 percent, of employees say that the option of remote work is factored into job decisions, and 54 percent of office workers say that they would leave their current jobs, for a position that allows for more flexible work places. The number of people who work remotely has increased 140 percent in the past fifteen years, and this is one trend that will continue in spite of any back tracking that some companies are currently trying to do with recalling remote workers, because people who work from home are 24 percent more likely to be more productive and happy.[42]

More changes in the *future of work* include jobs augmented with artificial intelligence, replaced due to automation, and working side by side with robots. Robots taking over our

---

42 Dragomir Simovic, "The Ultimate List of Remote Work Statistics—2020 Edition."

world is a big fear. Our sci-fi visions have left us feeling vulnerable to a hostile takeover by the machines, and even if that isn't a realistic fear, a very realistic fear is that with advancements in artificial intelligence, virtual reality, machine learning, and robotics, people working will become obsolete. The good news is that most current experts say that the new work paradigm will be man and machine instead of an either/or situation. So, this is where the skill of adaptability will come to be necessary because not only do we have to deal with uncertainty about how things will be in the workplace but also the way our work will be impacted by machines. We may even have machines or robots as a key part of our teams, so there will be new paradigms for working with them.

What we need to keep in mind is that while machines may be able to bring together patterns and connections in quantifiable terms far more easily than humans, when it comes to connecting people and recognizing their capabilities and capacity for innovation, machines just aren't as effective. For now, the machines are limited to highly specialized functions and there isn't going to be any sort of mass replacement of humans in the workplace.

Navigating through these new initiatives, causes, and pathways of work requires the modern worker to be adaptable to new situations while staying focused on the end goal. Especially given all the fears about losing jobs to machines, there is a lot of uncertainty in the workplace and most likely there will continue to be as we adjust to this new type of world.

"Change brings uncertainty, and for many people, uncertainty is terrifying."

One of my favorite quotes is by Bill Watterson, creator of the *Calvin and Hobbes* cartoon. Calvin and Hobbes are staring up at the vast sky and musing, *"day by day nothing seems to change, yet pretty soon everything is different."* I love this quote for the great truth it holds. Think about your life one year ago. Are things exactly the same? The answer will always be no. Change isn't always of magnitude, rather it can be made up of small changes. Either way, we tend to adjust to changes that occur over time. However, when it comes to large changes or changes that need to be implemented quickly, many people find it difficult because they either tend to ignore it, the proverbial *"stick their head in sand,"* or another technique is to use past experience to help navigate such situations.

Using past experience serves as a good baseline, especially in reminding one's self that this too shall pass, but what will serve us and our children more is developing the ability to adapt to change. We all have to live with uncertainty to some extent because we don't have magic wands or crystal balls to tell us what's coming our way however, as a certified change management practitioner the greatest challenge, I see, in managing change or uncertainty is getting people on board with the idea of change. As human beings, and thus creatures of habit, we get used to things being a certain way.

Looking at the current workplace trends, the gig economy, remote work, and the uncertainty surrounding new jobs in the Fourth Industrial Revolution, adaptability will be a very necessary skill to navigate differing contexts and unknown entities because the non-linear path of employment requires embracing lifelong learning. People who are adaptable or who have honed that skill have a curious and open mindset, which serves them well. Adaptability is essential because those who have honed in on the skill will not only be able to handle multiple contexts and situations in a different way but also have the mindset to approach things with curiosity which helps them deal with the uncertainty surrounding what the workplace will look like in the future.

DEVELOPING ADAPTABILITY

The skill of adaptability in self and adaptability in life—to be able to assess the context and be able to figure out how to mold yourself, if needed, to adapt to that context is a key competency. We need to emphasize for the youth that adaptability does not mean that one has to accept anything that comes along the way without question, but it does mean that you are emotionally less triggered and that when there's a problem, you don't focus on the problem endlessly, but instead look toward finding a solution. It means that you can remember what is within your control and how to react and manage what is not in your control.

- One way that we are naturally developing the skill of adaptability for remote work is that over six million Americans are pursuing online education. Moreover, nearly a third of all college students take at least one online course, and in 2018, approximately 20 percent of students pursuing online education identified as lifelong learners.
- Encouraging our kids to be curious and build on that curiosity is a way to develop adaptability. By exploring and gaining knowledge, children are introduced to

different contexts which expands their thinking and viewpoints. Learning and staying aware about what goes on in the world around them also helps them acclimate to change instead of feeling like change has blindsided them.

- Another way to develop the skill of adaptability is to not be afraid of asking questions and asking for help. We don't have to do everything on our own. We can also leverage technology to help us in unfamiliar contexts like Ms. Sethi did during her volunteer trip to Turkey.

- Taking risks or pushing yourself beyond your comfort zone is another way to develop adaptability. When my kids wanted to try different sports or activities, we encouraged that interest. However, as we know, children lose passion quickly when they don't succeed or sometimes because they don't feel comfortable reaching beyond their comfort zone. So, the only rule we had was that once our kids committed to an activity or an endeavor, they had to complete the commitment.

- Much like resilience, staying positive and reframing the narrative also helps in building adaptability. Instead of trying to cling to how things have always been done, experimenting and looking at things as an opportunity also builds the trait of adaptability.

CHAPTER 5:

CRITICAL THINKING

———

Our world was turned on its head with the COVID-19 pandemic. Besides the radical changes it has brought to our personal and professional lives, it has also highlighted that as a species, we seem to be losing the skill of critical thinking; the very thing that separates man from animal. Critical Thinking is a top ten skill for the *future of work* according to the world economic forum. In the interviews that I conducted with educators and business leaders critical thinking was number three on the list. Any report or list with skills for the future has critical thinking listed on it. Yet, this crisis has illustrated how much we have lost when it comes to thinking critically.

First, the conspiracy theories surrounding the pandemic. Unexpected and profound events tend to inspire conspiracy theories, but with the pandemic, we may have reached new heights. I am sure that everyone has read some variation of how this is caused by a particular technology, or that it is designed to be able to install computer chips into people and control our lives in that way. Second, the healing solutions proposed to control the virus range from eating certain herbs, consuming particular drugs that have shown limited to no efficacy, or ingesting cleaning solutions. Third, the attitude that many people had, especially at the start of the pandemic as things were developing, that because old people were targeted by the virus (which has since been proven false) young people and others didn't have to worry. Hence the high numbers of college students on spring break and people not taking social distancing seriously. Many more examples are found of how this pandemic has highlighted the lack of critical thinking in our society and globally; all of which are troubling.

"Critical thinking means taking in information, analyzing it objectively, and then making a reasonable decision based on the information."

ROBYN RUSSO, PROFESSOR OF ENGLISH
NORTHERN VIRGINIA COMMUNITY COLLEGE

When people say that people no longer think critically, they seem to be referring to the latter parts of the critical thinking definition, which is *"analyzing information objectively"* and *"making a reasonable decision."* They take everything they hear to be completely true, and if we take a look at the events that unfolded in the pandemic and afterward, it is evident that this is a widespread problem.

In the essay "The World is Fucked and I'm Pretty Sure It's the Internet's Fault" by Mark Manson, he writes, *"...when you give the average person an infinite reservoir of human wisdom, they will not Google for the higher truth that contradicts their own convictions. They will not Google for what is true yet unpleasant. Instead, most of us will Google for what is pleasant but untrue.*"[43] He illustrates this further with giving examples of how we can confirm our worst thoughts and biases and writes that *"the fact that I'm most easily given the information that confirms my fears and quells my insecurities—this is the problem."* I agree with Manson's thoughts wholeheartedly, and it's not to say the Internet is the reason why we no longer think, but it does point to a key factor as to why critical thinking is underdeveloped.

Moreover, since the Internet does have all kinds of information available, critical thinking is a crucial skill. Again, as referenced above, the divisive state of American media and politics is furthered by the misinformation that we all have access to. And since it is so readily and instantly available, it is even harder to analyze information objectively. There is a reason why the Nigerian Prince scams still collect approximately seven hundred thousand dollars per year even though they have been widely debunked.[44] Not to mention that there are other scams and hoaxes that people fall for. This is not to say that lack of critical thinking is the only reason why people get scammed, many of the cons are very sophisticated and convincing, but it does indicate that we need to pause and reflect on what we read on the Internet. Manson hits

---

43 Mark Manson, "The World is Fucked and I'm Pretty Sure It's the Internet's Fault."

44 Megan Leonhardt, "Nigerian Prince Email Scams Still Rake in Over $700,000 a year—Here's How to Protect Yourself."

the nail on the head saying that the fact that we can confirm our biases is not a good thing. The more we spend time with people who are like us, who think like us, and who espouse the same thoughts and beliefs, the more polarized we become socially, but lose that ability to analyze objectively and come to a reasonable decision. Besides the fact that the Internet provides a safe haven for every conspiracy theory, or ludicrous thought, it also provides the answers and information for pretty much everything. My first instinct is to turn to *"Dr. Google"* anytime I have a question. So, even if we think we're searching for objective responses, our tendency will be to confirm our own biases.

One blow to our education system for developing critical thinking was the legislation titled "No Child Left Behind" that was in effect from (2002-2015). Because of the rise in standardized testing, students were taught to focus on the one correct answer even though as they grew up in the age courtesy of the Internet, the knowledge of the world was available to them. Moreover, because school funding was tied to the performance on these standardized test scores, for many teachers and schools the only option became to teach the skills associated with good test taking, which are not the skills that promote critical thinking. As an ex-college professor, I know that we had to unwind that thinking of *"one right answer"* and try to get students to examine other alternatives. However, it's hard to undo that kind of thinking developed over twelve or so years in one semester or even an academic year.

In the book *Thinking Fast and Slow*, Daniel Kahneman describes our two systems of thinking, system 1 and system 2.[45] System 1 is fast, unconscious, and automatic. It also is error prone. System 2 is slow, conscious, and deliberate. It is used for analysis, problem-solving, and reflection. Even though we think we spend more time in system 2, system 1 is easier mentally (less load) and we tend to spend most of our time engaged in a system 1 type of thinking. Kahneman writes:

"Systems 1 and 2 are both active whenever we are awake. System 1 runs automatically, and System 2 is normally in comfortable low-effort mode, in which only a fraction of its capacity is engaged. System 1 continuously generates suggestions for System 2: impressions, intuitions, intentions, and feelings. If endorsed by System 2, impressions and intuitions turn into beliefs, and impulses turn into voluntary actions. When all goes smoothly, which is most of the time, System 2 adopts the suggestions of System 1 with little or no modification. You generally believe your impressions and act on your desires, and that is fine—usually.

When System 1 runs into difficulty, it calls on System 2 to support more detailed and specific processing that may solve the problem of the moment. System 2 is mobilized when a question arises for which System 1 does not offer an answer... System 2 is activated when an event is detected that violates the model of the world that System 1 maintains."

For the most part surviving in system 1 is fine, except for the fact that it likes to fit things into a coherent story, and it operates on limited information. So, when we go online

---

45   Daniel Kahneman, *Thinking Fast and Slow*, (24).

or when we talk to people around us who are similar to us, system 1 keeps reaffirming what we already know, then we don't engage in system 2 where the deeper thinking happens. Critical thinking which requires us to analyze information objectively, and make a reasonable decision. This does not happen with system 1 kind of thinking. To be a critical thinker; we need to challenge ourselves beyond that system 1 thinking. Beyond that single correct answer. We need to engage in the more thoughtful and reflective heavy thinking of system 2 where we challenge our assumptions. We can't do that by constantly forcing our youth to think toward a correct answer. If we want critical thinking skills to flourish, we need to take away an emphasis on standardization.

In Seth Godin's education manifesto, *Stop Stealing Dreams: What Is School For?* he posits the question "What is School For?" and lists four answers (he acknowledges that these are just a few of the responses to the question).[46]

1. To create a society that's culturally coordinated
2. To further science and knowledge and pursue information for its own sake
3. To enhance civilization while giving people the tools to make informed decisions
4. To train people to become productive workers.

Though we'd like to think that it is all of these and other more idealistic answers, the sad truth is that the way schools were designed and remain, the only thing they are accomplishing is trying to mold children into compliant and

---

46 Seth Godin, *Stop Stealing Dreams: What is School For?*

obedient workers who depend on their boss to tell them exactly what to do, which is frustrating to the bosses. As I write this, I know there are some of you who are thinking... *well it can't be all that bad, because, well, the bosses came from somewhere and so we must be doing something right and we are a leading nation in the world.* However, the reality is that we aren't.

The Organisation for Economic Co-operation and Development, 2018 Programme for International Student Assessment (PISA) results illustrate that the United States is slightly above average in reading and science, and below average in mathematics.[47] And though the reading scores in PISA were above average, the National Assessment of Educational Progress (an American test given in fourth and eighth grades) showed that two-thirds of American children were not proficient readers. The PISA test also highlighted that the achievement gap between high and low performers was widening in the United States. And though the US showed above average scores in contrast to other peer nations, in math, the US was below average with peer nations. Note that for the majority of the peer countries English is not the primary language and while being above average is merit worthy when put into context, it really isn't, especially since about a fifth of American fifteen-year olds have not mastered reading skills for ten-year olds. One rather optimistic thing to take away from the PISA report is that students who demonstrated a growth mindset by disagreeing or strongly disagreeing with the statement *"Your intelligence is something about you*

---

47 "OECD Ilibrary | PISA 2018 Results (Volume I): What Students Know and Can Do" 2020.

that you can't change very much" scored fifty-eight points higher than students who agreed or strongly agreed with the statement. Students who demonstrate a growth mindset not only benefit in the tests and studies they complete now, but they are also the ones that will be successful in the *future of work* as they re-skill, up-skill, and take on new roles and opportunities.[48]

Another interesting finding of the 2018 PISA report was that even those students who did not perform well on the test, still expected to go on to college and gain a college education.[49] More than 75 percent of low performers expected to finish college, which suggests that the linear education and the career path that we have been emphasizing to our youth has sunk in. While we ought to applaud the high expectations and standards that they are setting for themselves, at the same time what we need to be thinking about is how are they going to do well in this new type of world they are entering. A world where a college degree will matter at first, but will also demand that they keep learning. College is no longer the end of the road for education. And even if it were, these are students underperforming on this international standard of tests at the age of fifteen, and they are just a few short years away from entering college, an expectation that they have, but what kind of college experience are they going to have? What troubles me, and should be troubling all of us is that even if we're preparing our youth for the old

48 "OECD Ilibrary | PISA 2018 Results (Volume III): What School Life Means for Students' Lives" 2020.

49 "OECD Ilibrary | PISA 2018 Results (Volume I): What Students Know and Can Do" 2020.

model of a linear career trajectory that follows a linear education path of Kindergarten through twelfth grade, then a bachelor's, followed by a master's. What does it mean that in an international benchmarking test, our students are overall slightly above average in science and reading but below average in math. If they're not being set up for success in the old model, one that more closely aligned with the old workplace expectations, then how will they fare in the new workplace expectations.

On the other hand, the students who answered questions in a manner consistent with a growth mindset are the ones who will be able to achieve success in the new non-linear education and work pathways of the world. Because they view intelligence as mutable, they are also more likely to be receptive to new ideas and new opportunities. They are also likely to challenge their assumptions, all part of the system 2 type thinking. A key aspect of up-skilling and re-skilling is knowing how to learn what requires the reflection or the deeper cognitive thinking of system 2. This is something that I saw severely missing in my community college classroom. It was amazing how many students don't know how they learned. And it's not just the lack of preparation—showing up to class without books, papers, or pens. Though, certainly I would question how they expected to learn without the materials they needed. Granted there were many excellent students, but it still amazed me that there were students who were there to learn but didn't know how to learn.

So, one of the activities that I routinely did in my class was have students not only reflect on learning styles, but also think about when and how they learn best. Questions such as, did they learn better in the morning or at night? Did they need quiet or did they need some noise? Did they do better alone, or did they do better in groups? How did they take and organize notes? How long did it take them to learn something? How did they maximize their learning time? At the community college, the majority of my students had family and work responsibilities in addition to school. Sometimes simply by suggesting they take their reading with them to do on breaks at work, or the recommendation to get the audiobook and listen while they did housework or drove was also another way to receive the information and was a revolutionary idea.

Some of these cognitive skills that aid in learning have to be taught or instilled in our youth. They need to know how to learn as well as what to learn. In fact, a Stanford Researcher found that students who reflected on how they prepared to learn and how they learned best, helped them perform better on tests. As adults, we already know how much we benefit from planning and reflecting on our own thinking and learning. Therefore, it makes perfect sense that engaging in these kinds of metacognitive functions will help our youth in developing the critical thinking skills that employers are looking for. Also, as they go through this new model of education and work that is part of Industry 4.0, having this growth mindset and these cognitive behaviors will serve them well as they up-skill and re-skill.

Innumerable things need to be done to improve our schools, and a good place to start is deemphasizing the need for standardized tests. Humans are not standardized. We don't even have standard clothing sizes across all stores. If there is anything that takes away our ability in critical thinking (as well as our love for learning), it is being tested to death on things. Especially, since Dr. Google is at our fingertips, and we do have access to pretty much all the information in the world. We should be emphasizing what we do with the access to that information. Skills like evaluating the information or synthesizing complex things to demonstrate understanding or analyzing information to look at things from a different perspective. These are all parts of being a critical thinker and what helps us be better problem solvers. The need to slow down and focus on our thinking, engaging system 2 of our brain, and taking a pause before jumping into something, these are all actions we can take to develop our skills and help our kids as well.

The Fourth Industrial Revolution will demand a lot more cognitive flexibility from its workers. It's an executive function that we already need to have in our workplaces. It will be even more important in future workplaces as we try to figure out new work paradigms. Cognitive flexibility, sometimes known as flexible thinking is the ability to think of multiple concepts at the same time, to disengage from one task, and focus on another task. Cognitive flexibility is what allows us to think creatively and come up with different ways to approach problems. So, when we're looking toward developing these critical thinking and problem-solving skills, we should help our youth develop their cognitive flexibility. Getting our children to develop flexible thinking and thinking about how they learn will be essential tools that will help them in the re-skilling and up-skilling revolution they will be a part of.

DEVELOPING CRITICAL THINKING

In this world where we are inundated with information, pausing, reflecting on, and analyzing the information is very important. Unfortunately, because we are also in an age of instant gratification and we emphasize speed, many people sacrifice the time that it takes to pause and analyze for the sake of being expedient. Nevertheless, it doesn't have to be an either/or proposition. Developing critical thinking early will help it become more instinctual, and so in some ways they will gain speed. However, the greater thing we need to emphasize is the value and importance of this skill regardless of the time it takes.

- Literature is a great tool to develop critical thinking skills because it can help kids make observations and analyze information. When reading stories, children make inferences, they form opinions, and they make connections between their world and what's in the stories. All these activities build critical thinking because kids are taking information in and evaluating it and making predictions based on it–the essential definition of critical thinking.
- One way that Kindergarten through twelfth grade schools can really help build the skill is by doing more interdisciplinary projects or studies. In the workplace, employees typically don't work in isolation. Teams, departments, and divisions are all interconnected. Very few jobs have a singular focus, so learning how to make connections across disciplines and exploring things from different angles is vital to developing the skill.
- Instead of giving answers to questions all the time, encourage them to reflect on what they think the answer might be. Ask them what they think the answer might

be. Follow that up with why they think that way, or how do they know that to be true? Having them make connections and think things through instead of constantly being given the answer will help them learn to think for themselves.

- As children grow into teenagers, encourage them to be critical of their ideas, beliefs, and assumptions. Have them figure out why they think the way they think. Simultaneously, have them explore contrary ideas and beliefs and instill the activity of perspective taking in them, so that they don't fall into the trap of confirmation bias. Have them try to make arguments from the opposite side to help them look at information from a different point of view.

CHAPTER 6:

PROBLEM-SOLVING

——

Warren Wright, CEO of Second Wave Learning, who is an expert in characteristics of generations says that the tagline for Gen Xers (b. 1965–1980) would be the Nike slogan "*Just Do It*" because this was the generation of the latch key kids, and the generation that was generally left to their own devices to figure things out. As the lyrics in the infamous song "*Ice Ice Baby*" by Vanilla Ice say, "*If there was a problem / yo I'll solve it.*" This would describe this generation which is now currently in the middle of their careers, the oldest being around fifty-five years of age. So, it's no wonder that when they are interviewed about the younger professionals in the workplace today, so many of them lament over the millennials' lack of problem-solving skills. The term that I heard most frequently used was "*deer in the headlights.*" And of course, as all generalizations go, it does not apply to everyone in either of the generations, but employers in general feel that there does seem to be that shift in the workplace where young people are looking for explicit directions and guidance as to how to do things, rather than just getting things done.

We seem to have gone from a generation that took something and figured out how to do it or get it done to generations that want the entire map in front of them. So, no wonder employers feel that problem-solving is a missing skill in the workplace. And like critical thinking, complex problem-solving is a top ten skill needed for the *future of work* as stated by the World Economic Forum.[50] So, what exactly is it that employers want to see as demonstrating problem-solving? Merrilea Mayo, COO of Social Tech says that what most employers are looking for in their entry and mid-career level professionals are *"people who have broad problem-solving tools are able to figure things out. What the employers don't want is someone who says 'I don't know how to do this. Show me how to do this every single time.' That just consumes the boss's time, and he has his own work to do."* Mayo further adds that as employees move further along in their careers, or those in very technical and specialized careers, there is a requirement for complex problem-solving or the *"academic type expertise"* they have learned in school. However, basic problem-solving techniques like trial and error, looking things up on the Internet, finding and calling a local expert, taking an object apart to look inside, or rereading the instructions are good starting points because they help prevent the types of *"paralysis"* that employers see. What employers seek now, and what leaders say is needed for tomorrow is for employees to have enough of an understanding of problem-solving so that they can work independently. Because as Mayo points out, if the boss has to teach everything to the employee, then that employee is

---

50   Alex Gray, "The 10 Skills You Need to Thrive in The Fourth Industrial Revolution."

not worth it for them because they're adding more of a load than doing their job.

There are problems and there are complex problems. Regular problems can be complicated, but they are different than complex problems. Complicated, simply means that it's a challenging problem to solve. There may be many moving parts to the solution, or it may be something that is tedious and takes a long time to solve. However, problems, even complicated one's, typically follow five basic steps of problem-solving:

1. Define the problem.
2. Come up with alternatives.
3. Examine and select a solution.
4. Implement the solution.
5. Reevaluate as needed.

The problems that we face in the Fourth Industrial Revolution, though challenging and at times complicated, will be more complex. Complex problems don't necessarily have a tried and true solution. If we refer to the critical thinking chapter, specifically Daniel Kahneman's research on system 1 and system 2, complex problem-solving requires the system 2 type of thinking. However, there's a bit of a paradox, which is that complex problems require system 2 thinking, which is slow and deliberate, but at times the solution will need to be found quickly. Nevertheless, complex problem-solving usually requires finding multiple possibilities or approaches. This is the intersection of innovation, and often involves multiple people, teams, industries, and disciplines to find possible solutions.

One of the more popular and effective methods for complex problem-solving is design thinking. It's a process that has been around for a while, but it has had a recent resurgence. The broad steps of design thinking are to understand the problem, explore several possible solutions, iterate, and implement. While this sounds like any number of problem-solving techniques, what sets design thinking apart is that it is focused on and involves the end user. In understanding the problem, it requires that one immerses themselves in the problem, which is to say that if you don't have firsthand knowledge of it, you go out and gain firsthand knowledge by speaking to the users for whom you're trying to solve the problem. Because the tendency is to approach the problem from one's own perspective, that leads to a false understanding of the problem. And in exploring solutions, one brainstorms all kinds of possible ideas no matter how wild and crazy because sometimes the solution is in one of those wild and crazy ideas. In the iteration phase, prototypes are built, tested, and feedback is collected—the process is repeated until the solution is designed correctly—after which it is implemented. Design thinking is not something that is applicable in every situation, but it can be helpful to address the complex problems that we are facing in this new era of work.

How many of you hate making multiple trips from the car into the house? We have seen the memes of people unwilling to make two trips to get the bags out of the car. We have experienced the pain of lugging in heavy things from the car or taking things out to the car. One great example of design thinking is the innovation in how to open car trunks.[51] In

---

51   Adam Leon, "3 Great Examples of Design Thinking in Action."

2012, the Ford Motor Company introduced the *"foot-activated liftgate."* We have all had that experience of having our hands full as we approach our cars, only to have to put everything down to open the trunk. Add in inclement weather, and it can be disastrous for either the person carrying out the items or the items themselves. For safety and security concerns, the latch is only activated when the key fob is in close proximity and cannot be triggered by bumps in the road or animals.[52] By adding this feature Ford was the first car company to solve this problem for its customers. They took a universal problem and because they had firsthand knowledge and understanding of the problem, being car drivers themselves, they were able to come up with a solution that was focused on the user.

Another complex problem-solving method is systems thinking. In systems thinking, a person looks at the overall patterns and structures in a system, instead of seeing specific parts. By looking at how the entire system works and is interconnected, one can identify the pain points in a broader sense, and the problem can be addressed. So, it is a much more holistic point of view because it's not looking at a problem in isolation. As a process, systems thinking requires an understanding of the system as a whole and about understanding how each piece contributes to the whole before finally deciding how to approach a solution. Because of a broader look at the system, the solution is also more holistic because instead of focusing on fixing the problem within the system, it looks at all the parts that are connected in the system and their interactions with each other. It fixes the system to prevent the issue from

---

52   C.C. Weiss, "Ford's New Kick-Activated Tailgate Provides Hands-Free Opening."

reoccurring as opposed to a small piece of it. It's like Dr. Daniel Kim, founding publisher of The Systems Thinker™—a newsletter that helps managers apply the power of systems thinking, and co-founder of the MIT Organizational Learning Center says, *"Working **on** the system as opposed to **in** the system is a key lesson about systems thinking."*[53]

One cool view of systems thinking is demonstrated by Princeton University, which recently, displayed a series of portraits of the blue-collar workers at the university. Mario Moore, a former student of Princeton, is the artist behind the paintings and he painted ten workers at Princeton from facilities workers, to maintenance and dining hall employees.[54] He wanted to showcase the blue-collar workers and pay tribute to their work as his own father worked blue-collar jobs to support Moore's family. His work was purchased by the Princeton University Art Museum and the University was excited that they would become a *"permanent part of the University's collection."* While the paintings are not a response to a problem, they do offer a new perspective on the working class and racial struggles at the Ivy League college. The portraits provide a step toward thinking about everything and everyone that helps the university run the entire system. And at an Ivy League, where the majority of students are coming from privileged backgrounds, the portraits bring to light another aspect of society, and is contributing positively toward a discussion of the larger problems or race, entitlement, empowerment that are part of our society.

---

53 Daniel Kim, "Introduction to Systems Thinking."

54 Cathy Free, "Portraits on Campus Lacked Diversity, so this Artist Painted the Blue-collar Workers Who 'Really Run Things.'"

Divergent thinking is another way to approach complex problem-solving.[55] Divergent thinking is a method used to create many possible solutions through brainstorming. The ideas tend to be free flowing and non-linear. The concept of there's *"no wrong answer"* applies when using divergent thinking, as does *"thinking outside of the box."* Research indicates that as children, we are highly capable of divergent thinking because we haven't yet had to limit our answers to the *right* answer. As mentioned in the previous chapter, standardized testing and the general goal of helping students get to the correct answer, takes away the ability to think of alternatives. It also defies the concept of *"no wrong answer"* because students are always seeking the correct answers in school. That's what they are taught to do because there are concrete and defined goals for students in school curriculums.

The opposite of divergent thinking is convergent thinking, which is thinking in a linear and systematic way. We place a good deal of emphasis on convergent thinking in school, work, and life. People who are divergent thinkers view things in a different way. In 2019, Maurizio Cattelan, an Italian artist, created his piece *Comedian,* and it was displayed at an international art fair, the ArtBasel in Miami Beach. It was the most talked about piece of artwork in 2019 and achieved Banksy level status because of how unique the piece was.[56] What was the art about? It was a banana duct-taped to a wall. Prior art pieces by Cattelan include an 18-karat solid gold toilet–fully

55   Stacey Goodman, "Fuel Creativity in the Classroom with Divergent Thinking."

56   Sarah Cascone, "Maurizio Cattelan Is Taping Bananas to a Wall at Art Basel Miami Beach and Selling Them for $120,000 Each."

functioning–titled *America*, and *L.O.V.E.* a thirty-six-foot tall white marble sculpture of a hand with only one finger–the middle finger–sticking up as if giving the bird. Cattelan is clearly no stranger to creating unusual art, and while his work continues the debate over *"what is art?"* his artwork also illustrates divergent thinking. Because while convergent artists stick to norms, divergent artists give us new perspectives like the cubist and impressionist art movements.[57]

Design thinking, systems thinking, and divergent thinking techniques are good for the complex problem-solving, but as Mayo stated, employers are looking for some of the basic problem-solving techniques. XQ institute is an organization that was founded to help support educators, students, and families to reimagine high school education, and in one of its blog posts, the XQ team emphasizes that students should be taught to *"think like a scientist"* and learn the scientific method (observation, measurement, hypothesizing, testing, and modifying) as a problem-solving technique.[58] Other basic techniques that Mayo mentioned in her interview are trial and error. She also encourages asking questions to understand the problem and examine it from multiple perspectives before going into brainstorming and trying to find solutions.

Some other basic strategies for solving problems are analytical problem-solving, using facts and logic or other substantive experiences to find solutions, or using the fishbone

---

57 Rhett Power, "Give Divergent Thinking a Chance to Solve Your Biggest Challenges."

58 Larry Berger, "What do Young People Need to Learn Today to be Prepared for Tomorrow?"

analysis to figure out causes and effects surrounding a problem to find the solution. Be it a basic technique or a complex technique, problem-solving requires deep thinking, and for that we need to prepare our youth to be comfortable in questioning the status quo and looking at things from multiple angles. This is a point that we will need to emphasize and develop especially given that schooling is so focused on finding the correct answer to a problem.

Other important things to remember when it comes to problem-solving is that sometimes time is a necessary factor. Setting something aside for a while and coming back to it later can be an effective technique, as can sleep. It makes no sense to stay awake endlessly to try to figure out something, especially if you're stuck. Sometimes we get stuck in the loop of looking at something for so long that we need a break to help refresh and reset our brains. Quite frankly, sometimes we just need to give up on the problem and that doesn't mean to let it be. But often when we are stuck in the mode of here's the problem and let's figure out the solution, sometimes we need to step back and see if the problem really is a problem. Maybe it is a problem or maybe it was a random occurrence, or something that has been inflated into a problem. While the first step in problem-solving is to identify the problem, sometimes before even classifying it as such we need to see if it is indeed a problem.

DEVELOPING PROBLEM-SOLVING

Just like critical thinking, creativity and curiosity also lie at the heart of developing problem-solving skills. Sir Ken Robinson's TED Talk on "Do Schools Kill Creativity?" in which he makes the case that the current education system kills creativity,[59] has over sixty-five million views as of April 2020. As I have mentioned previously, this is not a teacher flaw but rather a system flaw. So, how do we help our children develop their problem-solving skills?

- Emulate and help kids learn the five basic problem-solving steps. In defining the problem, help kids break down the problems into chunks and help them follow the steps through until they find the solution. Don't forget to follow up with them when they have put their solution in place to see how it worked out.
- Strengthen their research skills. As Merrilea Mayo shared in her interview, employers want employees who are proactive in finding solutions and not going to the boss every time they run into a problem. We need to teach our kids that asking for help is okay, but first we need to teach them to be independent enough to try and find solutions. Test a couple of things out before we turn to our boss.
- Bolster their decision-making skills. Sometimes it's hard to solve a problem because of an inability to decide or to act upon a solution. This is where resilience comes in as an important skill to help them. Because the fear of making a decision or implementing a solution is a fear of failure, helping them become resilient helps them move away from inaction.

---

59 Sir Ken Robinson, "Do Schools Kill Creativity?" Filmed February 2006 at a TED Conference, TED video, 19:13.

PART II:

DEVELOPING
PEOPLE SKILLS

Jean Paul Sartre wrote, *"Hell is other people."*

In the future of work, as we walk along the non-linear career paths one thing that will remain constant is interacting with people. And, unlike machines, humans don't come with instruction manuals. Each person is unique. Some people are easier to get along with than others. One skill that has always been and always will be crucial in professional and personal lives is being able to maintain relationships with others regardless of how challenging or difficult the person might be.

There's a picture of Scar from *The Lion King*, surrounded by his hyena pals, Shenzi, Banzai, and Ed, and there's the caption, *"I'm surrounded by idiots."* It always makes me chuckle because I think all of us have identified that sentiment at least once (a day). Yet, here we all are–sometimes surrounded by idiots; sometimes we are the idiots. Joking insults aside, sometimes so much of the work we need to do for our self is dependent on our relationships with people.

People are often disgruntled. They say, *"What's the point of self-awareness when people around you aren't?"* I contend that's all the more reason why we need to first work on ourselves because when others don't, at least we can manage our relationship with them and keep ourselves from being stressed or drained. As much as we fantasize about buying an island and living there with only the people we want, we're all bonded with each other and the complexity that is humanity. It's easy to say I have done my part, now everyone else should do theirs. However, sometimes that's not the case and when that happens, we need to be equipped with the tools to get through and get the work done. We need to do the same for our kids.

Empathy, negotiation, conflict resolution, teamwork, and innovation are all key people skills for the future of work. Korn Ferry Hay Group research found that human capital holds the greatest value for organizations now and in the future, despite the emphasis on technology in the future of work.[60] *"People, labor, knowledge—will be worth as much as $1.2 quadrillion over the next five years. In contrast, physical capital—inventory, real estate, and technology—will be worth an estimated $521 trillion. Human talent and intelligence are*

---

60   Distefano, et al., "The Trillion-Dollar Difference."

2.33 times more valuable than everything else put together."[61]
Therefore, developing essential people skills in our youth will give them an advantage for the non-linear career paths they will chart.

---

61   Kane, et al., "The Very Human Future of Work."

CHAPTER 7:

EMPATHY

—

When I asked Hunter Haines, Senior Organization Development and Inclusion Consultant, what advice would she give her five-year-old grandson about the one skill or trait that he should develop to be successful at work, her response was *"Be Kind."* It's the same advice she says his mother, Haines' daughter-in-law, gives him. Haines further elaborates that *"being kind sends other people signals that they can trust you, and that they can let their guard down with you."* How you display that kindness when people may not know you well is *"through being genuine, by listening openly and without judgment, smiling, and showing empathy."* And though constantly smiling at work is not feasible, having a positive non-verbal affect lets other people know that you're receptive to them.

"Be Kind" is one of those phrases that is constantly bandied about by people, but we shouldn't treat it lightly because everyone can agree on the fact that the world can never have enough kindness. And just as Haines and her family emphasize this value to their newest member, we too can instill this value. Kindness is inherent in being an empathetic person. Empathy goes hand in hand with kindness. Empathy is

defined as the ability to understand and share the feelings of others, and the first step toward fostering good relationships with other people. Kindness is the quality of being friendly and considerate. Kindness comes naturally when directed toward our loved ones, but when we step out of that circle and deal with the rest of the world it can be harder. Humans are tribal in that we will always protect our own against others. And that has served an evolutionary purpose, but in today's world, we are all interconnected and dependent on one another, so the us versus them can be a real detriment to our society. That is where empathy can help us manifest kindness toward others.

There are three types of empathy.[62] Cognitive empathy, which is understanding the perspective of others, emotional empathy, which is understanding how others feel, and empathic concern, which is caring for others. I like the division of empathy into these three types because cognitive and empathic types of empathy allow for individuals to understand what the other is going through without having first-hand knowledge of the experience because we can't have experience in everything. In my opinion, empathic concern is the most basic form of empathy, and if it isn't already intrinsically present, it is a skill that can be most developed. Cognitive empathy is the next level up and is inclusive of empathic concern. Emotional empathy is all-encompassing and the highest level of empathy that can be achieved. By breaking empathy down, it allows for children and adults to demonstrate this at a level where they are comfortable.

---

62 Dona Matthews, "Empathy: Where Kindness, Compassion, and Happiness Begin."

Because realistically speaking, we can't expect that everyone will become emotionally empathetic because if our natural instinct is to protect our tribe, then it comes at the expense of others.

The early stages of the COVID-19 pandemic are a great illustration of the us versus them mentality, and why we need to emphasize empathy as an important trait now and for the future. Some people started hoarding cleaning supplies, hand sanitizers, face masks, and gloves when the first rumblings of the pandemic reached the United States. *The New York Times* wrote a story about two brothers, Matt and Noah Colvin who *"cleaned the shelves"* of hand sanitizer and antibacterial wipes at the big box stores in Chattanooga, Tennessee.[63] And while Noah drove around Tennessee and Kentucky and stockpiled these items from all the stores that he could get them from, Matt waited for large shipments—pallets of wipes and hand sanitizer. He sold them through amazon for anywhere from eight to seventy dollars per bottle more than he had paid for them. They were purposeful in their purchases and were looking to *"put (their) family in a good position financially"* but at the expense of others' wellbeing. Retail arbitrage is not new.[64] In fact, there are many people who research best-selling toys in advance of the holiday season and stockpile those and sell them at higher than retail prices. But in the case of the pandemic it extends beyond just trying to earn some extra cash. Because they and others who engaged in similar behavior of stockpiling essentials deprived people from

---

63   Jack Nicas, "He Has 17,700 Bottles of Hand Sanitizer and Nowhere to Sell Them."

64   Greg Besinger, "The Web's Most Maniacal Bargain Hunters."

purchasing these items during a time where it is a matter of life and death.

Then there were the people who were stocking up, or rather hoarding, basic supplies like toilet paper, milk, eggs, and other basic foods and necessities. They were definitely in an extreme survival mode of taking care of themselves and their own tribe. Granted, a pandemic is something that we haven't experienced for several generations now, and in living memory of the world, so the *"fight or flight"* mode was perfectly reasonable. And while such people were not engaging in profiteering off the pandemic, these people did behave in a selfish manner because people's extreme stockpiling left other people who are food insecure or on really tight budgets in a lurch as they went to the stores and found them empty of foods they needed. When we're part of a society, we have an obligation to the people in our society. It's the old philosophical nut of social contract theory, which is that when we are part of a society or community, we all implicitly agree to abide by the rules of the society. So, while there's no written agreement or rule about having to take care of others, we *have to* for the greater good. Because when we take care of the people in our communities, it also helps us. So, even though it is natural to want to take care of ourselves and our families and loved ones first, we cannot shirk our community and societal responsibilities. Even in a pandemic... especially in a pandemic.

Displaying emotional empathy can be hard for many as it really asks people to reach in deep to their emotional core and understand how they might feel in that situation. Not everyone is in touch with their own feelings or self-aware, so asking them to understand how another person feels can be asking too much. The mindset of *"suck it up and deal with it"* stems from this because if that's how you handle emotions in your own life, then you're not going to have the patience or willingness to understand it from the other person's perspective. Forty percent of American adults suffer from loneliness.[65] For instance, we all have the experience of being the new person in a situation. Starting a new school, new job, meeting new neighbors, people, or whatever the situation may be. Being the new person brings a level of anxiety for all of us, and when it comes to starting a new job it can be isolating to not have a person to eat lunch with or to be part of the inside jokes, and so on. Most companies have done a decent job of having some sort of onboarding so that the first couple of days, new employees are introduced around and have a person to go to lunch with. This is a demonstration of emotional empathy—understanding that starting something new can feel overwhelming. Ultimately, when companies discuss onboarding procedures, they're trying to help their new employees fit in with minimal distress of being the new person and that is because their leadership is emotionally empathetic.

One step below emotional empathy is cognitive empathy where you may not be able to feel how the other feels, but at least you understand their perspective. One very powerful way that some people have demonstrated cognitive empathy in the times of the pandemic is that leading up to and at the start of April, in the midst of the initial stockpiling of food and goods, there were a lot of reminders on social

---

65   Bruce Lee, "Cigna Finds More Evidence of Loneliness In America."

media to encourage people to check food price labels and if a label was marked WIC, to not purchase those items. That's because WIC is the Special Supplemental Nutrition Program for Women, Infants, and Children, and if those items are not available, then the people receiving the benefit can't substitute another item for purchase. So, the people who originally created the message demonstrated emotional empathy. People who shared the message at least had empathic concern, and people who forewent an item or items they wanted or needed to allow others to benefit displayed cognitive empathy. If emotional empathy seems out of reach or seems like an unlikely personal goal, then developing this skill to the point where you can at least understand the perspective of the other person is achievable.

At the very minimum we need to have empathic concern—care for others. We're not the only ones experiencing a traumatic event, it's the whole world…literally. Even though we may feel panic or emotionally spent, we need to extend our concern beyond our own self. Many people display empathy and show care and concern for others. From young children who are collecting supplies to share with front line people or contributing their own money toward helping others in need to adults who are volunteering their time and energy and helping those who are at risk. One of the people I interviewed, Logan Deyo, who is an incredible person all round, took the time to establish a text-based system where at-risk residents of Richmond, Virginia can ask for help with groceries and other tasks and volunteers can assist them. Many people are already informally doing this for friends and neighbors, but Deyo's system expands it to the general area. It also utilized a method that generally all people are comfortable with because even the elderly presumably are familiar with basic text messaging. However, it turned out that the elderly were not as adept at texting, so Deyo opened it up to voice requests also to better serve the needs of the community.

Empathy is a key skill in today's workforce, and one that we should all possess or work toward because demonstrating empathic concern gives us a better understanding of our clients' needs or the needs of our co-workers, supervisors, or employees. Fulfilling the needs of our clients or customers makes us a better employee, and often there are rewards and recognition tied to employee performance. That's an immediate benefit for us. But looking ahead to the future, empathy is an important skill for the *future of work* because it is quintessentially a human skill. Employing empathy can make challenging situations with people easier to navigate because by taking the perspective of the other person even if you can't feel what they feel, or you don't even care about them too much.

In the future of work, artificial intelligence and automation can replace or enhance the *"hand"* and the *"head"* types of work, but they cannot replace the *"heart"* type of work.[66] People who *"want to stay relevant in their professions will need to focus on skills and capabilities that artificial intelligence has trouble replicating—understanding, motivating, and interacting with human beings. A smart machine might be able to diagnose an illness and even recommend treatment better than a doctor. It takes a person, however, to sit with a*

---

66 Maria Delgado, "The Path to Prosperity: Why the Future of Work is Human."

patient, understand their life situation (finances, family, quality of life, etc.), and help determine what treatment plan is optimal.[67]" And the shift to such *"heart"* type of work, will require a greater need for us to connect and build a rapport with others. With automation of some jobs and the fact that man and machine will work side by side in the future of work, there are chances that a person may do some jobs isolated from humans. Given that humans are naturally social individuals already and so many people experience workplace loneliness, it's important that we develop and maintain connections with others and to react and respond based on the context of the situation, for which we will need to improve our empathy skills and emphasize building empathy with the youth.

Anti-bullying campaigns in schools heavily emphasize the value and virtue of kindness, and there's a reason for that. We must encourage and guide the youth to pay attention to the dynamics around them. Be the person that stops others from bullying. Be the person that sticks up for others when talking to others. Be the person that refuses to say anything negative about another person (or say anything they wouldn't say to the person face to face). Be the person that makes friends with the kid that is new or alone. Be the person that looks around and pays attention to how people are showing their feelings. Because when we emphasize behaviors that remind our kids that other people exist and that others matter too, we're helping develop that empathic concern, the very base of empathy.

---

67 Megan Beck and Barry Libert, "The Rise of AI Makes Emotional Intelligence More Important."

Moreover, the rules of empathy should extend beyond in-person interactions to online conduct and communication too. Too many people are spewing hate and vitriol in the comfort of anonymity. Though the illusion of anonymity fools us all; the truth is there isn't total anonymity. People can be connected to what they post, what they write, in many different ways. For the majority of us that might mean that if we write something spiteful, it only impacts that reader(s) at that moment, but for some of us that might prevent us from achieving a goal or for our mistakes to come under the spotlight. Not to minimize the distress that we cause to other people by thinking we have a veil of anonymity, but there are also natural consequences to bad online behavior. We witnessed this in the early days of social media when job offers were rescinded based on applicants sharing personal thoughts and behaviors. Granted these were not anonymous, and they were open for anyone to see but with a little sleuthing, things can be connected to the original posters. The Internet never forgets anything, and nothing is truly anonymous. So, whatever our kids post or use to represent themselves, we must ensure that they know it reflects upon their overall character. And if you hurt someone anonymously, it's just as bad as hurting them in person. Anonymity shouldn't be an excuse to be mean or unsympathetic. If anything, I think we could all show more empathy online.

In the midst of a pandemic, we have seen people who have indulged in extremely selfish behavior and we have seen incredibly selfless behavior, but in the midst of it all have been the majority of the people who have had to adjust so much of their lives, and that includes children. The fact that their school year ended abruptly, and they were not able to see friends and families they saw on a regular basis, these are two very radical shifts in their lives. An April 18, 2020 post on the Instagram account @scarymommy said *"My son just brought me soup in bed and my favorite neck pillow because I wasn't feeling great. Honestly, I don't care if he does all of his homeschool assignments because at the end of the day, if he is showing empathy and compassion, he's learned a lot more than he could ever learn from a damn computer."* We don't yet know how the pandemic will impact the kids in the long run. But I agree with the @scarymommy post that if all they learn is empathy and compassion, they'll be fine.

BUILDING EMPATHY

Developing emotional empathy can be hard. Some people may have a difficult time understanding the emotional state of another person, especially if the individual is not emotional themselves. So, to have a three-tier approach to empathy allows for people to display the skill in different ways without feeling like they lack the skill completely since they cannot match the emotions of others. To recap, the three types of empathy are: cognitive empathy—understanding the perspective of others; emotional empathy—understanding how others feel; and empathic concern—caring for others. Nothing captures the essence of empathy as does the golden rule. Treat others the way you want to be treated. We all try to live by it and certainly get upset when we feel others aren't honoring it in our favor, but we can all do better about treating others as well as we would treat ourselves.

- One of the main ways to develop empathy is through stories. Fiction can help in developing all three types of empathy. By listening and reading to stories of others, we can instill a sense of curiosity for other people. And if we are curious and eager to learn more about others, it broadens our perspectives, and we can improve our cognitive empathy. Stories of adversity can broaden emotional empathy because we tend to identify with, and root for the main character, and if we take our children on a journey with the character, they can refine their emotional empathy.

- Another way of building all types of empathy is being part of a community. It doesn't matter if it's religious, ethnic, family, friends, neighbors, schools, or personal interest. When children (all ages) are connected to adults other than parents, they benefit from such relationships because they have more people to turn to when they need help. Also, with the diversity of communities, our youths build cognitive empathy and empathic concern, which will increase emotional empathy.
- Set clear expectations. In the school atmosphere, be clear that you expect kids to care of one another and the entire school community. Talk about it, model it, praise it, and hold students to it! Just don't pay it lip service by putting it on a poster and expecting kids to internalize it somehow.
- We all tend to ask the children in our lives, *"How was your day?"* at the end of a school or camp day. We ask about how a certain activity was. We could switch up the question. Instead we could ask *"How were you kind today?"* or *"How did you show kindness?"* By asking them that, we're asking them to reflect on their behavior and think about whether they put this trait into action or not.
- Participate in planned and random acts of kindness yourself and as a family. I think we all engage in planned acts

of kindness through charitable giving and volunteering our time, and it's great for our kids to see that. As they get older, we should definitely involve them in the planned events. It's important for them to see how privileged they are. Random acts of kindness can be as simple as holding doors open for people as they exit behind you, paying for someone's coffee, smiling at everyone for the day, giving people compliments, and sending something through the mail just because.

CHAPTER 8:

COMMUNICATION

In the past couple of years, *"ghosting,"* a term used in dating, has been associated with employment also. According to Urban Dictionary, an online slang dictionary, in dating ghosting occurs *"when a person cuts off all communication with their friends or the person they're dating, with zero warning or notice before hand."* In the business world ghosting is something that employers are experiencing, for instance, when employees don't show up for interviews or even for their first day after they have been hired. When the employer reaches out to the candidate or new hire, they cannot get a hold of them. A fairly new phenomenon, fastcompany.com reported in August 2019 that approximately 83 percent of employers have been ghosted in the past couple of years.[68] After ghosting an employer, some people have asked others to call in *"dead"* for them—say that they are dead and that's why they didn't show up to the job.

Though in most cases, ghosting tends to occur at the start of the job, in a couple of rare cases, an employee stopped

---

68   Lydia Dashman, "The Latest Trend for Job Seekers: Ghosting Employers."

going to work after a difficult day at work. One water park manager, Kris, whose story was shared on NPR, ghosted his employer by not showing up to work to open the park on a busy day.[69] The company had promised him a raise when he was promoted to a manager position, but he never received it. After Kris regularly reported to work for a few months, the company announced that they would be cutting employee rates for cost savings, so Kris ended up with more responsibilities and less pay. The day that Kris ghosted, the company was forced to keep the park closed because no one else could cover his responsibilities, which resulted in a loss that far exceeded the pay raise they had promised Kris.

Employers and recruiters have been ghosting employees for a long time. We all have a story of sending in a resumé or having an interview, only to never hear from the employer. It's a terrible feeling; especially after an interview since most of us have to take time off our current job to interview. Ghosting is not just an American problem. In Japan, there is an industry created around helping people resign.[70] The consultants will type up resignation letters or make resignation phone calls on behalf of their clients. They will also negotiate any time off or money owed to employees. In Japan, it has more to do with the cultural expectation of not quitting because quitting is considered a bad habit. Nevertheless, it highlights the challenges of dealing with people especially with difficult or awkward situations.

---

69 Emily Sullivan, "In a Hot Labor Market, some Employees are 'Ghosting' Bad Bosses."

70 Bill Chappell, "For $450, this Japanese Company will Quit Your Job for You."

People can find it difficult to communicate especially in challenging situations with their bosses. In the case of Kris, he communicated to try and resolve the issue, but he didn't get the support he needed, so he felt that he needed to *"ghost."* Communication is the top skill in people skills that leaders feel is currently missing, and it's going to always be a vital skill for the workplace. But communication is a broad area, so business leaders narrowed it down to two areas where they felt that our youth could gain more experience. The first is to be able to negotiate between you and others—handle difficult conversations. The second is clear expression in writing. These were the two areas in communication they felt were most lacking and needed to be addressed.

DIFFICULT CONVERSATIONS

Those of us who are far away from those fun-filled days and nights of college wax poetic over how they were the best days of our lives. Those were the best days of our lives in many ways. If you think about it, it's one of the only times, if not the last time, we had complete control over our own schedule. Before that, our schedule was dictated by school hours and to an extent from our parents. Afterward, it has been dictated by our work schedules. Perhaps that autonomy is what we miss, but for many of us, and for a lot of our youth, that autonomy was or is hard to navigate because we're not used to it.

College is essentially the first opportunity to negotiate with people. Prior to that, our only opportunities are with family and friends and, due to the dynamics of those relationships, negotiation can be hard because with friends, we tend to compromise or do what it takes to fit in; with siblings, the power dynamic is such that there isn't a reason to come to consensus, and with parents, well, there may be some opportunity, but at the end of the day they are the authority, and at some point, parents pull that rank. College becomes the first opportunity to practice the art of negotiation, yet that is a skill that many young people don't know how to develop and don't have the opportunity to develop. Merrilea Mayo, COO of Social Tech describes the gap in negotiation as *"people have work to do at a specific event, you know...to be turned in at a certain time. And (sometimes) not only does it not get done when it's supposed to get done, but they (employees) don't tell anyone because they're afraid that they'll get punished or it'll be a difficult conversation."*

Therefore, one of the dynamics in the work world is that while there are some non-negotiable deadlines, and deadlines set by others, we do have the chance to negotiate those at times. Not always, but we do have ownership over our time to some extent. So, when the boss asks us to do something, and it is too much because of everything else that we have going on, then we have a chance to say to our boss, as Mayo says, *"I'm looking at my calendar. I'm looking at my workload, and there's no way this is going to get done in time, can we figure out an alternate strategy?"* But according to Mayo, so many of the younger employees are ill-equipped to conduct such a conversation with their peers, let alone their bosses because *"there's no communication exercise in school where you're sitting striking up a deal with a teacher about an upcoming deadline and trying to make things work...you know in school you just turn in your assignment, or you don't turn in the assignment. And then you beg for an extension after the fact. There's no proactive conversation about deadlines and responsibilities and making sure that things don't fall apart because for some reason you can't do your part."*

In college many professors do give this opportunity to students. I know that when I was teaching at the community college, I would tell my students that I recognized that we all had a life outside of my class, and that if they were having *"life drama"* and needed time, as long as they asked in advance of the deadline for extra time, nine out of ten times, I was willing to give it to them. Sometimes even on deadline days, if I had a student share that their kid was sick so they couldn't get it done, we'd negotiate when they could get it to me. I would say that 99 percent of the time, the time that students requested was reasonable—an extra twenty-four to forty-eight hours. This was a message that was in my syllabus, something that I said the first couple of weeks of class, each time an assignment was due, and each time I returned a graded assignment. Inevitably though, each semester, I would have at least one student who would not turn in an assignment, would promise to do so, but fall behind, and *"ghost"* on the class. Or there would be the student who would come to class, and participate and do really well but not turn in any assignments and when I would ask him or her why they were behind, the response would be along the lines of *"Well I never did the first one, and then I just didn't know how to get back on track."* With such students, I often had to deliver the painful news that because they had avoided talking to me for so long, they would now have to retake the class, which in this day and age of high college tuition fees was not something either of us wanted.

My experience as a professor was not in isolation. One of my old colleagues in the English department, Robyn Russo, PhD, shared the same sentiment. When I interviewed her, she shared how overwhelmed students get and *"when it comes to having to deal with any paper or assignments, whether that's with a classmate (peer review), or whether it's going to a professor and asking for help, or to say I don't understand this, it becomes overwhelming for them."* While difficult conversations are not easy for anyone, why is it so overwhelming for young people? Russo suggests that it has to do with the fact that parents have always stepped in to solve problems, and in fact, she has received calls from parents to try and solve problems for their college student. She's not the only one. Several of my community college colleagues shared similar stories where parents wanted to intervene on behalf of their children, either for grades or to make up assignments.

Sadly, college is not the last place where the helicopter or snowball parents intervene on behalf of their children. The trend to shelter and protect them has also extended into the workplace. On the blog *Askamanager* by Alison Green, there are several stories of parents intervening in professional situations, such as parents who have tried to negotiate salary and benefits, parents who have called out sick for their kids, or parents who have called to find out the status of an application. By protecting our youth to this extreme we are not allowing them to develop this crucial skill of handling difficult conversations, and we are also lowering their capacity for resilience. As adults, our job is to allow our children to handle difficult things on their own and be there to help them, but when we start stifling them, then it's no wonder that they struggle.

WRITTEN COMMUNICATION

When I was teaching, I tried to maintain a friendly relationship with my students, and at the start of each semester, we would go over what is considered professional communication. I would share with them how to address the email and to include pertinent details like which class they were in and what times the class met, so I could differentiate between my students. I also let them know that I would respond to most emails within twenty-four to forty-eight hours. This rule was added after a couple of semesters when I realized that students expected instant responses and that they would wait until the last minute. So, at 3 a.m., I would receive questions about assignments due for the 8 a.m. class. Even after I established these rules, I would still have students who didn't follow them. The worst offender was a student who emailed me five times within fifteen minutes, the last couple of emails were just emojis. One was an email full of sad faces, and the final email was a string of the crying face emojis. I used that student's communication minus identifying information to illustrate what kind of emails not to send in the future.

I'm not the only one who expected professional communication from my students then or from employees now. Over and over, what I heard during my interviews with business leaders was that *people need to learn how to write.* There were expletives and sighs involved with that sentiment, but that was the gist of it. When I prompted them to explain why they felt that way, most leaders felt that their employees, especially the younger ones, could not write clear emails, let alone do more intensive business writing. One person said, *"They don't understand that writing to their boss is not the same as writing to their friends."* The chief complaint about their writing was being informal and using texting and slang language in professional communication. That was followed by an overall lack of clarity in written communication, especially when writing longer pieces like reports or proposals. I even heard a story about how one new employee couldn't even type up a meeting agenda.

Writing, like every other aspect of communication, is based on context—who is the audience? Personal communication is different than professional communication. Even if an employee has a friendly relationship with their boss, that doesn't mean that there shouldn't be any formality in email communication. Once upon a time, emojis were completely unacceptable in any kind of professional communication. Now people are a little more okay with it, but again it depends on the context. With co-workers, the rules are different than they are with the boss, department heads, or even other colleagues from different departments. Knowing when to differentiate your communication is an important skill.

When I taught, in both reading and writing courses, I would tell students that I could guarantee that writing a summary was something they would do at least once in their careers. It didn't matter what industry, or what type of job they did. At some point in their lives, they would have to write a summary. For anyone who hasn't written a summary recently, it's hard. However, summaries aren't the only types of writing that need to be done in the business world. More and more writing is being done at work in every business and industry. Employees spend nearly 3.5 hours a day on their work email alone.[71] And if they don't know how to communicate clearly, they are costing employers time, money, and resources. Think of all the back and forth emails you may have had to have to understand the other person or to explain yourself to others.

Nearly three-fourths of employers want employees with strong written communication skills, and it's the number three desired skill behind leadership and teamwork.[72] Employees have to do many types of writing now that won't be changing in the near future. Digital marketing is an important part of every company's branding and that requires content. Some companies have content writers or people on staff. Others who have the budgets outsource it. However, most companies try to use in-house talent. With more and more content online, being a good writer can be invaluable because you can help build a strong business presence and reputation. That's not all. Employees in all companies will have to partake in business writing for presentations. Plus, reports and proposals are also something that employees frequently must write.

The ability to write well is not only good for effective communication, but also it makes a difference when it comes to differentiating one's self from others. Because employers rank this skill so highly when it comes to being competitive for jobs, if you have strong writing skills, it will separate you from the rest of the applicants. Many people feel that if

---

71 John Hagel, John Selly Brown, and Maggie Wooll, "Skills Change, but Capabilities Endure."

72 Kaleigh Moore, "Study: 73% of Employers want Candidates with this Skill."

they're in a certain industry or type of job, they don't need to have strong writing skills. Writing skills are not only indicative of being a good communicator, but also that you are able to organize, analyze, and synthesize information. Being a good writer separates you from the rest of the pack because it illustrates your ability to be logical and persuasive. If you can be persuasive, that will get you more business.

The emphasis on standardized testing has minimized the emphasis on developing writing skills. Even when students have to write for tests like the SATs, there are robo-graders that can read and score some essays, and the grading is based on the technical aspects of writing and does not leave any room for creativity. An NPR story covered this issue a couple of years ago, and in it Les Perelman, MIT research affiliate, found that grammatically perfect essays scored perfectly even when they made no sense.[73] Perelman generated a five hundred-word essay with sentences like *"History by mimic has not, and presumably never will be precipitously but blithely ensconced."* Grammatically error free, but no real meaning behind them. Students have figured this out, so they have exploited the weakness of such systems. With most disciplines not requiring essays or other types of writing, students are not able to practice the skill enough, which leaves them at a disadvantage. We need to incorporate more writing across our education curriculum.

There will be jobs that will be automated in the future of work, and the Fourth Industrial Revolution will mark a workplace

---

73 Abigail Hess, "Here's How Many Hours American Workers Spend on Email Each Day."

that will be augmented by artificial intelligence, which is why human skills are so important. Writing is still one of those skills that has not been mastered by AI yet, and a soft skill that is becoming a part of more and more jobs.

DEVELOPING COMMUNICATION SKILLS

DIFFICULT CONVERSATIONS

Being able to have difficult conversations with others effectively is a key skill, and one area where our youth doesn't get enough experience in is negotiating—working things out with other people. This is mostly due to their age and the social orders we have set up in which adults are the authority. When children question authority, they are usually reprimanded or disciplined, therefore, they rarely get a chance to practice this skill.

Sibling relationships are typically fraught with rivalry and other complexities. Even when there is an opportunity for negotiation, if it doesn't work out, it can devolve into classic sibling power struggles. Such negotiation is typically missing from friendships because like sibling relationships, friendships have their own dynamics. One of the reasons why it's hard to practice this in personal relationships is because there's empathy and concern, so people tend to *"make nice"* sooner than when they are dealing with colleagues or supervisors. With bosses, there's the demarcation of authority and with colleagues there's a line between friend and foe, so difficult communication is fraught with a lot of emotion.

- As the adult, or people in authority, where possible, give children the opportunity to practice negotiating. This works with older elementary aged kids and beyond, but it's an important skill to practice. Maybe it's negotiating about bedtime, or maybe it's negotiating over screen time. Hear them out and help them practice this. Encourage the same kind of negotiation between siblings and friends.
- One of the elements of negotiating is being able to manage multiple responsibilities. In this modern world, our kids are definitely managing multiple responsibilities, but parents step in and intervene. I understand the desire to step in and take care, but instead use this as a moment to help your child learn how to balance their responsibilities. Encourage them to talk to their teachers and find alternatives.
- As they become teenagers, give your kids opportunities to interact with individuals in positions of authority around them. Have them take the lead in conversations with their doctors at the checkups or talk to their coaches if they have team or sporting issues.

WRITTEN COMMUNICATION

Being able to write well is a skill differentiator from other employees. It is also an indicator of an intelligent and credible professional because it demonstrates strong logic and persuasion skills.

- As I mentioned above, there needs to be more writing across the curriculum because interdisciplinary work is important in developing critical thinking and in helping develop strong writing skills. Schools should stop minimizing the need for writing and find more ways to include it.

- Developing many of the soft skills requires self-awareness. Introspection, and journaling is mentioned as a tool for developing those soft skills. Journaling is a way for them to practice their writing skills too. So, encourage this practice for a boost in several soft skills.
- We should also encourage them to hand write instead of typing because research has indicated that taking notes the old-fashioned way is better for us cognitively.

CHAPTER 9:

TEAMWORK

When I was teaching, the two scariest words I could say in class were *"group project."* Many memes about group projects accurately convey the pain that they can be. Group work or projects in school are the precursor to teamwork and collaboration in the workplace, and most teams are bogged down with conflicts or dysfunction. Nevertheless, however problematic it may be to work in a team, it is an essential component of school and work. Collaboration is already a key element in the professional world, and its importance will not diminish in the future of work. Group dynamics however, will continue to shift radically as more and more people work remotely, or as temporary workers move in and out of jobs, and we can't forget that as we enter the future, man and machine will work in partnership.

Not all teams are dysfunctional and, in fact, when a team works well together the results are quite spectacular. A plethora of research has been found as to what makes a good team, but what stands out amidst all the findings are those from Google's Project Aristotle, which studied maximizing teamwork over a five-year period. Project Aristotle found that "*a great team features a mix of the right intangible char-acteristics.*"[74] And when it comes to teamwork, how the team works together turned out to be better at determining success, rather than who was on the team. The five characteristics of great teams (in order of importance) according to Google's Project Aristotle are: psychological safety, dependability, structure and clarity, meaning, and impact.[75]

These team traits that make up stellar teams are closely linked to the key skills listed in this book. Psychological safety is linked to empathy, because empathic individuals show concern for others, so they will allow for their teammates to share ideas without fear of being judged. This provides psychological safety and allows each team member to feel valued and able to contribute to the team's goals. Dependability is easy for the individual who is good at holding themselves personally accountable. Through effective communication, team leaders can provide the structure and clarity needed to ensure that all the members of the team are on the same page and understand the directives so the goal can be accomplished. Empathy is also critical for fostering meaning—showing gratitude and appreciation to everyone involved in the team.

We all like to hear compliments, and genuine recognition of good work bonds the team through promoting a sense of purpose. Finally, resilience and communication are key for

---

74 Charles Duhigg, "What Google Learned from Its Quest to Build the Perfect Team."

75 Elle Kaplan, "Google Found the Most Successful Teams Share these 5 Traits."

recognizing the impact of the team. Too often some of the work that is done by teams, despite interdepartmental colleagues making up the team, is done in a silo. It can be easy to let the challenges or setbacks derail the spirit, so resilience is essential to keep moving forward. When team leaders couple resilience with communication, they help keep their team motivated through these challenges by reinforcing how the team's contribution impacts the company's goals.

Dom Price, the head of Research & Development at Atlassian Corporation Plc, shared in an Entrepreneur article, "*the future of productivity is all about unleashing the potential of your teams.*"[76] According to Price, "*Ninety percent of organizations claim to be tackling issues so complex, they need teams to solve them.*" But in the *future of work* teams will look different in two ways. More collaboration will need to be done online because of telework, remote work, and globalization. Also, the *future of work* will most likely have teams or groupings of people *and* robots. What will the team dynamics in such eventualities be? That aspect is uncertain, but it is important for our youth to consider these possibilities and to become familiar working in tandem with machines. So, because teams will be different, teamwork will also need to be handled differently.

The COVID-19 pandemic has turned the workplace virtual. Everyone is doing their best to accommodate the various circumstances under which people are working, but such compassion is not sustainable. Soon we will either have to

---

76 Martin Welker, "The Future of Productivity: Teamwork and Collaboration."

adjust to this as a new normal, or we will return to some hybrid form of work, and that is when people will begin to have the expectations of productivity and the type of work that used to be the norm. If this is the new normal, then soon we will need to have everyone trained to work remotely including collaborating virtually. Even if near remote work is not the new norm, the pandemic has illustrated that we don't always need to be in an office. Even prior, to the pandemic, approximately 50 to60 percent of employees felt that they could do their job remotely, and 80 percent of employees want to work from home at least some of the time.[77] Regardless of whether it is now or a few years from now, remote collaboration will continue to be an important skill that teams and individuals will need.

Teamwork, in real life or in person, is challenging enough as it is, so when there is an element of virtual distance, then it becomes even more challenging. However, the same principles of what makes great teams apply whether the team is virtual or in real life. An *MIT Sloan Management Review* article, states that for virtual teams, *"social skills,"*—being good at teamwork,[78] has to be a prerequisite when creating virtual teams because the farther the physical distance between team members, the greater the virtual distance is. If it's possible, face-to-face meetings allow for more effective teamwork, so if companies can afford the expense of getting the team together, it's a worthwhile investment.

---

77 Adam Hickman and Jennifer Robison, "Is Working Remotely Effective? Gallup Research Says Yes."

78 Frank Siebdrat, Martin Hoegl, and Holger Ernst, "How to Manage Virtual Teams."

One thing I asked some of my interviewees, was when did they learn teamwork? A couple of people said they learned it by being part of group sports or, in one case, a theatre group in high school and college. But besides being coached on playing or being told how to act, they didn't recall specific activities or directions on how to behave as a team. The same went for group assignments in school. Group projects are a key part of school because the goal is to help students learn to work in teams. But when assigning groups, teachers either do it randomly or allow groups to form on their own. Many teachers *"assume that students will figure out how to work together."*[79] I know that during my teaching days, when I assigned group projects, I expected students to figure out how to work together on their own. Granted I was doing that with my adult college students, so I felt the higher expectations were warranted.

Even in Kindergarten through twelfth grade, some teachers try to facilitate successful teamwork through establishing group roles, but others do not. When there are moments of conflict and certain team members who don't contribute their share, more often than not, teachers still penalize the entire group for the mistakes of one. Some teachers, me included, deal with the "unfairness" complaint by assigning separate grades for the group and for the individuals. However, teachers should add some explicit instruction and group facilitation to help kids who may not have the skills to work well together. Developing this key skill for our children, requires teachers to be more active facilitators when assigning group work.

---

79   Jami Back, "Teaching Students How to Work Together."

Another way to get better results from teamwork is to keep a group together as a team long-term.[80] Once they build that bond, the team becomes closer to developing or develops some of the characteristics that Google's Project Aristotle found to be part of great teams. So, if there are several group projects throughout the year, it would be worth it to keep the same teams for the whole year. In virtual teams, often the focus is on getting the job done as opposed to building relationships. Team bonding outside of the project or work is important for the success of the team. The informal interaction that takes place helps promote the psychological safety within the team. This is one of the reasons why team sports dynamics change when a new player or players are introduced.

A Deloitte white paper on "Transitioning to the Future of Work and the Workplace" states that *"Communication, collaboration, and connectivity are at the core of much of what the C-suite believes will drive the major changes in the future of work."*[81] For the longest time, email has been used extensively for collaborating, coordinating, and connecting employees. In recent years, with improved Internet and more cloud-based programs, there are plenty of ways to connect and collaborate.

"Now, we're entering a new phase of collaboration where team members can use tools to speed up innovation, jumping from

---

80 Amber Messersmith, "Preparing Students for 21st Century Teamwork: Effective Collaboration in the Online Group Communication Course," 223.

81 Stephen Redwood, Mark Holmstrom, and Zach Vetter, "Transitioning to the Future of Work and the Workplace."

the boardroom to their personal devices while keeping the conversation going via video and messaging apps to finish the job, even when they're not in the same office or time zone—this is the future of work," says Joe Berger, Practice Director for Collaboration at World Wide Technology, a global technology provider and systems integration business.[82]

Similarly, most schools have some kind of online learning software or apps. Schools use either Google classroom or some other form of learning management systems, or a combination of both. These tools provide virtual collaboration opportunities, but just like in real life, we need to teach our students how to use these effectively. A study that focused on preparing college students for virtual collaboration indicated that initially technology was frustrating, but eventually students were able to see how they use technology differently and for different purposes. They were able to see how technology could be used to collaborate in the workplace and by using it they also shared *"plans to incorporate applications into their personal, academic, or professional lives."*[83] So with online collaboration, it all comes down to training students and employees on how to use it and what to use it for.

When there is talk of man and machines, most people conjure up visions of robots that they have seen in sci-fi movies or as described in sci-fi books. They imagine armies of human-esque robots rendering people obsolete at work or

---

82   The Workplace of the Future.

83   Jane. S Prichard, Lewis A. Bizo, and Robert J. Stratford. "The Educational Impact of Team-Skills Training: Preparing Students to Work in Groups," 136.

taking over humanity and becoming overlords. I asked a friend who's in the field of robotics whether robots will ever become sentient and take over humanity, and he said in his professional opinion no. Because ultimately, it's human intelligence that creates these machines, and while there are ways that machines develop intelligence, they can only do it in specified realms as opposed to the breadth of cognition and experiences and innate characteristics that humans possess. So, robots will not be taking over our jobs or us, they will however be helping us in our jobs.

Thomas Malone, Director, MIT Center for Collective Intelligence describes four types of human-computer collaboration. The first level is where computers are tools, and we're already at that level in our daily work—where we use computers to do what we want them to do. The examples he shares of computers as tools are using computers for word processing or for spreadsheets. The next level is assistants where computers do some of the simple or easy to automate work so humans can work on some more complex or contextual work that requires more of a judgment call, such as what we might see in basic level of customer service through chatbots. The third level is that of a peer, and the last level is where robots are the managers. We have yet to completely achieve either of these two levels in a way that replicates or replaces humans, and whether we will achieve it or not is yet to be seen. One thing Malone emphasizes is that machines have specialized intelligence, where they can be programmed to do better than humans in a specific context like IBM's Watson that beat human players on *Jeopardy*, as opposed to the general intelligence that humans possess, which can be used to achieve a myriad of goals in a variety of situations.

What's interesting to note, however, is there is no clear definition for robots, and even roboticists have different ideas about what a robot actually is.[84] One definition the IEEE, Institute of Electrical and Electronic Engineers, presents is that *"a robot is an autonomous machine capable of sensing its environment, carrying out computations to make decisions, and performing actions in the real world."* They further explain that robots typically do three things: sense, compute, and act, and while there's a variation in the capacity of what different robots can do, they all act on a feedback loop where they sense information, process and compute the information, and then act on the information. Robots are constantly repeating the sensing-computing-acting cycle to become smarter and more efficient.

While we worry about robots taking over, we are already using robots to do work that is *"dull, dirty, and dangerous."*[85] We have robots that are used for bomb disposal, and the military uses drones for surveillance. Robotic arms are used in manufacturing as well as robots that weld. There are robots that assist with surgery. So, humans are already working in tandem with robots. One thing we need to keep in mind is that:

"Robots are not automatically capable of teaming with humans. They need to be assigned effective roles on the team, understand other team roles, train with human team members to develop common understanding, develop an effective way to

---

84   Erico Guizzo, "What is a Robot?"

85   Major General Mick Ryan, "How to Plan for the Coming Era of Human-Machine Teaming."

communicate with humans, and be reliable and trustworthy. Most importantly, humans should not be asked to adapt to their nonhuman teammates. Rather, developers should design and create technology to serve as a good team player alongside people."[86]

So maybe instead of teams of humans and machines, we might just continue to work in tandem with them—robots have their part and humans have their work. We also have jobs that are augmented by AI, and the next frontier is human beings augmented with machines, an area that the US military is working on.[87] For now though, there are jobs where humans are aided by AI machines and robots, and though the fear that jobs are going to be automated en masse are valid, it's also important to remember that there are many jobs that have already been automated. Jobs like travel agents are almost entirely obsolete except for a very niche market. With the rise of self-checkout lanes in the retail sector, soon the job of cashier will become obsolete. However, note that for self-checkout machines, there is a cashier or supervisor of machines who is there to assist customers if they run into difficulties, an example of man and machine, and also an illustration of how machines may cause shifts in the types of work people do.

I think it's important for us to remember how we learned teamwork because unless you're actually on a team, sports or otherwise, with whom you spend time training, playing, winning, losing, most of us learn along the way by seeing

---

86 Nancy Cooke, "Your Next Colleague could be a Robot. Here's how to Get Along."

87 Nancy Cooke, "5 Ways to Help Robots Work Together with People."

what works and what doesn't. Some of us don't learn. The five characteristics of great teams (in order of importance) according to Google's Project Aristotle are: psychological safety, dependability, structure and clarity, meaning, and impact. Key traits of good team members are individuals who contribute to those five characteristics of great teams. So, when people are honest, empathetic, responsible, focused on the team goal, and supportive in their team projects, they are contributing toward the success of the team. The soft skills of empathy, communication, and conflict management in this book contributes to developing our youth with the right skill set for being good team players.

DEVELOPING TEAMWORK SKILLS

Since school group work is the precursor to teamwork, as adults we need to ensure that we guide our youth on how to work within a team and as a team.

- Families can participate in team type activities. For instance, parents can assign projects like spring cleaning, sorting through donations, having a garage sale, family meal planning for the week, family weekend activities, and so on. Each child can be assigned different projects to lead, and as the team leader they are responsible for achieving what success looks like.
- If you conduct any sort of family meetings, those are a good time for kids to take the lead and conduct the meeting. They could also do a team-building exercise at the time.
- Help the youth foster the five characteristics of teamwork individually, but also teach them to bring these traits to

their groups when collaborating and promote them in teamwork.

- For virtual teams, have a channel or space where people can participate in more informal conversation. It's a good place to check in with a question or quote of the day; or my personal favorite which is sharing memes.
- Also, as we have seen during the pandemic, many people have been hosting virtual happy hours. This should be a practice that should continue where teams can have a BYOB meeting or chat session. Other ways to unite virtual teams are through having book clubs or watching and discussing shows. The pandemic is teaching us the value of staying connected and of finding creative ways to do that. We should continue doing so even when it's not a must.
- Encourage children to have a basic understanding of artificial intelligence, and how to leverage that. This is something that will be necessary not only from the perspective of teamwork but also in general for the future of work.

CHAPTER 10:

CONFLICT RESOLUTION

———

In a 2018 article in *The Atlantic*, "A Shocking Number of Killers Murder Their Co-workers," author Rene Chun wrote that the third largest cause for workplace deaths were homicide, and the three biggest reasons were love triangles, fraud, and disgruntled employees.[88] Disgruntled employees or ex-employees have killed people for reasons such as fraud they committed, about to be discovered, or disagreeing with the other person's politics or they weren't doing a task correctly. It used to be that the majority of the workplace homicides occurred during the course of a robbery, however, that is changing because in 2011, 51 percent of workplace homicides were due to robberies, and that number fell to 46 percent in 2015.[89] At the same time, however, the number of non-robbery homicides increased during that time from thirty in 2011 to fifty-one in 2015, and according to the most recent statistics published by the US Bureau of Labor Statistics (BLS) on injuries, illnesses, and fatalities in 2017, there were seventy-six

---

88 Rene Chun, "A Shocking Number of Killers Murder Their Co-workers."

89 Doucette, et al., "Workplace homicides committed by firearm: recent trends and narrative text analysis."

workplace homicides.[90] There aren't definite statistics from BLS for 2019, however many media outlets like the *LA Times*, NBC, BBC, and others reported that the number of deaths from mass killings hit an all-time high in 2019, with a total of forty-one mass killings (defined as the death of four or more people), of which thirty-three were mass shootings.[91]

On May 31, 2019, an ex-employee, DeWayne Antonio Craddock, started shooting at a Virginia Beach Municipal Center. As reported by CNN, Craddock had resigned earlier that day.[92] At the time of his resignation he was in *"good standing in his department"* and his *"performance was satisfactory"* said Virginia Beach City Manager Dave Hansen. And though the investigation didn't turn up a concrete reason for why Craddock went on his rampage, he had been reprimanded before and in the days leading up to the mass shooting, he had committed an error that he thought would cause him trouble. Craddock's co-workers, neighbors, and others described him as an *"average," "nice"* guy. When someone has anger, is narcissistic, or has psychopathic tendencies, a mass shooting, still abhorrent, is easier to understand. However, Craddock's case illustrates that is not always the case. We're all familiar with the phrase *"seeing red"* to indicate a sense of rage so strong that it blinds us from seeing any rhyme or reason. Even *"normal"* people can do stupid things during moments of anger. We need to teach our children (and adults)

---

90   "Workplace Homicides In 2017."

91   "U.S. Mass Killings Hit A Record High In 2019: 'This Seems to be the Age of Mass Shootings.'"

92   Darran Simon. "Virginia Beach Gunman's Resignation Email Hours before Mass Shooting Offers No Clues."

conflict resolution skills, so that a situation won't escalate to the point where homicide becomes an option.

Because of the amount of time we spend with our co-workers, interpersonal conflicts are bound to happen, and with the increasing polarization of ideologies in the United States and an uptick in workplace homicides, conflict resolution skills are going to be more and more important especially since workplace conflicts impact us personally, alters our work environment, and affects a company's bottom line.

ACCOUNTABILITY

Recently, I met a friend for lunch and as one does with friends, there was a lot of kvetching. Sadly, or rather realistically, much of the conversation was about work (because #adulting). Accountability, or lack thereof was something we discussed in great depth. Mostly, it had to do with the lack of accountability on the part of leadership, but we also did a deep dive into personal accountability. Accountability from leadership is something that we all yearn for and are quick to notice when it isn't present. In contrast, though there isn't enough thought given to personal accountability.

"We are very good lawyers for our own mistakes, and very good judges for the mistakes of others."

—UNKNOWN

Personal accountability is an important piece of self-management and in managing conflicts. You have to be able to acknowledge and be honest about your own mistakes as part of the cause of a conflict. Almost half of the business leaders I interviewed felt that personal accountability was an important skill missing in young employees in the workplace. They felt it was difficult for such employees to develop and succeed since they couldn't recognize their own mistakes and take accountability for their own actions that might contribute to an interpersonal conflict.

One of the reasons why accountability can be difficult to develop is because so many of us associate it with punishment, especially when we think that leadership is not holding employees accountable. We want there to be consequences when someone is not living up to their responsibilities. When I asked my interviewees about why there might be a lack of accountability with their employees or within their organizations, some of them responded they felt it was a challenge for them as a boss to walk the line between disciplinarian and coach. Another reason was because in organizational culture if there isn't accountability at the top, then it's hard to enforce accountability going down the ranks of the organization. When it comes to accountability in company culture, one thing that we can instill in our youth is to demonstrate accountability as they move up the ranks in their jobs.

Moreover, equating accountability to punishment is not the correct view of accountability. Again, the view we should all have is that we are raising our youth to be the kind of adults we want to associate with when they grow up. We should view accountability as a piece of mentoring or coaching rather than a one-time event. It is easier to see other people's shortcomings sooner than we see our own, and when we are in those positions as leaders instead of waiting for things to come to a head and then trying and failing to hold someone accountable, we should be helping the individual when we see the shortcoming surface and definitely before it becomes an issue. A *Harvard Business Review* article lays out accountability as a dial with five steps.[93] The first three steps are designed to coach the employee whereas the last two steps lead to more serious conversations surrounding probation and termination. Step one is to informally mention the issue with the employee. Step two is if you see a pattern emerging take the time to check-in with the employee to see if there is a deeper reason (personal stress or life) why they may be making the missteps that they are. Step three would be to have a conversation in which you would guide the employee and track their improvement. For leaders, this approach to accountability can help them in being the coach and mentor for their employees in addition to holding them accountable.

Personal accountability is an important competency for the *future of work* because of the growth that comes with it. New jobs, new roles, and new possibilities will exist, and as our children chart their way through the new way of approaching jobs and careers, they will need to have a growth mindset. Without developing a personal sense of accountability, their growth will be stunted thus, limiting their possibilities. Personal accountability is deeply connected to becoming more empowered because when you hold yourself accountable, you

---

93   Jonathan Raymond, "Do You Understand What Accountability Really Means?"

take ownership over your thoughts, actions, and attitudes. It's a hard process because it requires us to see our flaws and shortcomings, but if we can nurture this habit in our youth, they will find it easier to face the difficulties of life and will find it easier to be able to hold others accountable. A 2005 study found that children who were encouraged to take personal responsibility for their actions also had more positive social interactions.[94] Being honest and accountable to ourselves helps us in our relationships with others because if we find that there are challenges or issues in our interpersonal relationships, our personal accountability will not only allow us to recognize where we can improve but also to make our case with the other person and find the solution to the issue.

INTERPERSONAL CONFLICT

Even though there has been an increase in workplace homicides, the vast majority of people won't resort to extreme violence. Nevertheless, the uptick in violence is something we all should be concerned about because we spend nearly a third of our adult life at work. Like any other relationship, sometimes we dish out our negative emotions like anger or frustration on our co-workers or we receive it from them. When you spend so much time with other people, conflict is inevitable and dealing with conflict in a professional setting can sometimes be harder because it may occur in front of others; it may involve multiple people; it may involve power inequity. Also, the people we work closely with, for better or worse, become their own version of a family. And just like our biological or chosen family, we have a variety of different personalities,

---

94 "Developing Personal Accountability."

some easier to deal with than others. For the most part we have to find ways to deal with difficult people because cutting them out or walking away from a job is not always possible.

One of my favorite blogs to read on a regular basis is *Ask A Manager* by Alison Green. She gets asked the most interesting, tantalizing, and absurd questions about workplace relationships and issues. On November 19, 2019, she received a question about a workplace conflict in which two employees, part of a team of eight, refused to speak to one another.[95] In meetings, if one person in the feud would participate in a meeting, the other person would not. The manager who sent in the question, who was a recent hire, was asking for help on resolving the situation. Green's response was *"tell them it's unacceptable and needs to stop."* She further gave advice on how to speak with the two individuals, and one point Green makes to the manager is that it is a job expectation or even a requirement that in addition to the actual work that is a person's responsibility, people have to be able to have *"civil, cooperative relationships with coworkers."*

Effective conflict resolution is an important skill we can impart on the youth (and continue to learn ourselves). The first step to handling conflict is being able to hold ourselves accountable. We need to be able to see the part that we play in a conflict. That is why self-awareness and management are the first of the soft skills to develop. We should know whether we are the type of person who avoids conflict or the type of person who seeks conflict because by knowing ourselves in this manner we can see how our behavior impacts our

95   Alison Green, "Two of My Employees Won't Speak to Each Other."

conflict resolution skills. Avoiders will suppress their emotions, whereas Seekers will vehemently defend their point of view.[96] However, even with the best self-awareness and self-management skills, what we can do in a moment of conflict is, perhaps, avoid a scene. However, it doesn't actually solve the conflict that we might be facing.

Amy Gallo, author of the book *Dealing with Conflict* identifies four types of conflicts.[97]

1. **Relationship conflict** is due to a personality clash or over negative emotional interactions.
2. **Task conflict** is over the goal of the task.
3. **Process conflict** occurs over how to complete a goal or project.
4. **Status conflict** is over hierarchy or who takes the credit for the work that has been done.

Conflicts can and will straddle the four types or have aspects of all of them, but by categorizing them, it gives us an opportunity to get to the root of the issue because when there is a conflict both sides feel injured or disrespected. By trying to figure out the type of conflict it is can help with managing one's emotions and with finding a path toward a solution.

Empathy and time are two key elements of conflict resolution. Time allows you to move beyond the emotions of the moment and figure out the root cause of what is upsetting you. By categorizing the type of conflict as suggested by Gallo, it may

---

96   F. Diane Barth, "Are You Conflict Avoidant or Conflict Seeking?"

97   Amy Gallo, *Dealing with Conflict*, 4.

also help with formulating a solution. In the workplace or in school, cognitive empathy can be helpful because even if you don't care for the person or understand their feelings, you can stop and try to put yourself in their shoes. Gallo also shares four options as to how to deal with the conflict. The first one and most frequently used is to do nothing. The second option is dealing with it indirectly, which sometimes comes across as passive aggressive behavior, or a better option is to ask another person for help with it. The third option is to deal with the conflict directly, and the fourth is to *"exit the relationship"* as in stop being friends with the person or in the case of work find another job or transfer to another position.

There isn't a perfect way to solve a conflict. And try as one might, there is no way to avoid it completely because where there are people, there will be some conflict. And usually, we get through conflict, sometimes with hurt feelings or a bruised ego, and sometimes very calmly and easily. However, there is one thing to teach our children, which is that sometimes people who are seekers of conflict, for them being right is the only solution or win they will accept. When dealing with someone like that, it is important to remember that even if they are 100 percent wrong, it's not always important to be right. Such individuals usually desire the win and not to resolve amicably. Before it escalates into a violent or hostile situation; it is best to let it go. If it's a pattern with this person to handle conflict by stonewalling others, then that's a behavior that should be reported.

We spend at least a third of our life at work if not more, and we routinely have to interact with all different kinds of people. According to a 2008 study, nearly half of workplace conflicts are caused because of clashing personalities.[98] And such conflicts cost US companies *"$359 billion in paid hours"* and *"employers spend 2.8 hours of their workweek dealing with conflict."*[99] A study from 2018 found that 58 percent of employees leave companies because of negative office politics, and thanks to Glassdoor and other online review sites, 86 percent of workers won't apply to companies with negative reviews.[100] This may be considered more of a company issue and not an employee issue, but it becomes an employee or a people issue because it doesn't matter how stellar an employee is, if they cause conflicts or are involved in them frequently they lose their jobs. In a future where our human skills will be valued more, we need this highly important skill to keep ourselves relevant.

RESOLVING CONFLICT

ACCOUNTABILITY

One of the rules in our house is that if we make a mistake or we do something wrong, we own up to it because making a mistake is a fact of life, and we all make mistakes. Same with doing something wrong. Sometimes we have a lapse in judgment. Sometimes we get overly impulsive. These are normal behaviors for humans big and small. However, lying to cover up a mistake or a transgression is unacceptable. Now we're either doing something wrong to cover up a mistake or piling up another wrong on top of the first lapse in judgment.

---

98   "Workplace Conflict and How Businesses Can Harness It to Thrive."

99   Ibid.

100   "Your Best Employees Are Leaving. But Is It Personal or Practical?"

When it comes to accountability, what are we trying to accomplish? Accountability does not mean being punished for a mistake or a transgression. Accountability means taking responsibility for yourself, your actions, and your reactions. The key point with accountability is it requires clear expectations and consistency.

- Whatever form of discipline you choose, align it with what you're trying to teach them. For example, if a child breaks something of value, then what should they be accountable for? As an adult what would you do? You would apologize and try to replace the item. Therefore, hold the child accountable in a similar fashion.
- The same applies in schools. They should be held accountable for whatever error they make. If it means chronic late work, then at some point they have to be penalized for that (provided other factors have been accounted for.)
- Behaviorally, accountability ties in with emotional self-management. They are responsible for how they choose even after someone has wronged them or if they are just in a bad mood and something irritates them. Reactions are a key part of accountability as well.

MANAGING CONFLICT

Amy Gallo's four types of conflict are very helpful in trying to figure out how to resolve conflict. By introducing the concept in your own life, and in the lives of the kids, you provide them with a way to hone in on what exactly is upsetting them.

Below are the types of conflict again and ways to help the youth resolve them.

1. **Relationship conflict** is due to a personality clash or overly negative emotional interactions. Helping our youth acquire self-awareness and self-management skills can help with relationship conflicts. Also, teach them to remember things that they like or respect about the person they are in conflict with to help them change any negativity. Finally, it's helpful to remember that we have the choice of how we respond to the conflict.

2. **Task conflict** is over the goal of the task. The important thing in such a conflict is to be able to listen to everyone's input and find the way to complete the task. By listening to everyone's input, we make sure that the other person or people feel valued. And if there's no consensus, it's always best to get clarification on what the task goal is.

3. **Process conflict** occurs over how to complete a goal or project. Like a task conflict, getting everyone to share their ideas is helpful because allowing for everyone's input provides other perspectives and can provide the solution to completing the project or meeting the goal. Sharing perspectives helps people see the different ways and perhaps aids consensus on the best possible process.

4. **Status conflict** is over hierarchy or who takes the credit for the work that has been done.

All in all, there are essentially three ways to address conflicts. You can either let it go, you can address it directly, or you can change the relationship. The problem is that these are all difficult things to do, which is why conflicts escalate. Also, there are some individuals who thrive on the drama of a conflict. Identifying the type of conflict and teaching children how to address those conflicts builds their people and relationship skills.

CHAPTER 11:

DIGITAL SKILLS FOR THE FUTURE OF WORK

When I was teaching at the community college, I was one of the first faculty members on my campus to offer a blended learning course—we met in person for half the time and we met online for the other half. Over time, as the department added more blended courses, we also began to evaluate digital textbooks. Because of rising textbook prices, and to get students to truly adopt a blended course approach to learning, electronic textbooks seemed to be a panacea. They cost significantly less, and many came with online portals where students had access to additional practice exercises; however, it turned out that students hated them. Many of the students would print out these slim but still substantial, at one-hundred-or-more-page, textbooks. Even if I assigned a short online article, the majority of my students regardless of age and adeptness with computers, would print them out because they preferred the touch and feel of paper, and felt that it was easier to study from paper. I understand because I personally prefer paper over e-books, but still I was surprised by this attitude, especially among the younger students who had grown up with technology as part of their educational and personal lives.

These were the students who were born in the digital age. They'd had access to the Internet their whole life, and they were super active online in their social media networks and staying connected with family and friends. It turned out that digital skills for social purposes were significantly different than digital skills for academic purposes. Social networks were easier to navigate through than learning management systems (LMS), and the skills from one didn't translate to skills to the other. In retrospect, this seems obvious, but at that time it was somewhat puzzling. My colleagues and I thought maybe e-textbooks were harder because they were used to paper, and so it was just a matter of time to adjust to the new paradigm. What we didn't realize is that time is not the only factor when adjusting to new paradigms because digital learning required a different set of skills. I was at fault for thinking that switching to an e-textbook would also translate to success in online learning, no matter how many additional resources came with it.

Similar to the assumption that my colleagues and I made that social digital skills will translate into academic digital skills, as we enter the Fourth Industrial Revolution, we assume that because people are online and so immersed in technology, everyone will be digitally ready for the new chapter in human history. Unfortunately, that is not true. In a ten-question survey, conducted by the Pew Research Center, to test American's knowledge of a variety of digital topics ranging from cybersecurity to social media, only 2 percent of those surveyed answered all ten questions correctly.[101] The median number of correct answers was four, and for eighteen to twenty-nine year olds the median for correctly answered questions was only five. One would expect that this age group, which is comprised of younger millennials and Generation Zs, who have grown up with electronic devices in their hands and access to the Internet from a very young age, they should be able to answer all questions correctly or at least do better than 50 percent on such a survey.

Moreover, when it comes to workplace technology, there are multiple applications and systems that we all need to use for our jobs. For instance, Slack is one platform that many companies use nowadays. Their website defines it as a *"collaboration hub that can replace email to help you and your team work together seamlessly."*[102] Most companies have it in addition to email. Add in other software applications, and suddenly people have several avenues to coordinate with their team members. But 61 percent of employees feel overwhelmed by all the technology that they have to manage for their workplace.103 So, as we enter the Fourth Industrial Revolution, we need to prepare our youth with the digital skills needed for the future, but first we need to tackle digital literacy.

---

101 Emily Vogel and Monica Anderson, "Americans and Digital Knowledge."

102 "What Is Slack?"

103 Carrie Duarte, Dan Staley, and Bhushan Sethi. "Our Status with Tech at Work: It's Complicated."

President Trump issued an executive order in February 2019, Executive Order on Maintaining American Leadership in Artificial Intelligence, in which he declared[104]:

"The United States must train current and future generations of American workers with the skills to develop and apply AI technologies to prepare them for today's economy and jobs of the future."

However, before we can even get to skilling all future generations with AI skills, one major problem we face is the digital divide, which began with the Third Industrial Revolution, will continue and become exacerbated in the Fourth Industrial Revolution. The digital divide is the gap that exists between individuals who have access to modern information and communication technology and those who lack access.[105] The Federal Communications Commission just released a report saying that 21.3 million Americans, or 6.5 percent of the total population, lacks access to broadband Internet.[106] This number is contested by the company Broadband Now, which says that their research data indicates the number of American's who can't purchase broadband Internet is 42 million, which would make it approximately 13 percent of the population.[107] If a sizable number of Americans don't even

104 "Executive Order on Maintaining American Leadership in Artificial Intelligence | The White House."

105 Carmen Steele, "What is the Digital Divide?"

106 Federal Communications Commission, "2019 Broadband Deployment Report."

107 John Busby, Julia Tanberk, and Broadband Now Team. "FCC Reports Broadband Unavailable to 21.3 Million Americans, Broadband Now Study

have access to reliable Internet, then how are they supposed to be prepared for the Fourth Industrial Revolution.

Moreover, just having reliable access to the Internet isn't enough to develop digital literacy skills as evidenced by the aforementioned Pew Research Center survey.[108] A disparity is found between older and younger users of the Internet, as well as across the level of education attained by the individual. However, the results are still abysmal. Thirty-one percent of individuals who identified as having a college degree—bachelor's and up—didn't know that private browsers only prevent someone from seeing how you have used your computer and is not private from employers or ISP service providers. Similarly, only 47 percent of college educated adults know that a URL starting with https:// is a secure site, with a total average of 30 percent of all individuals who were didn't know the meaning of the 's' at the end of the http. Moreover, 17 percent of adults were unable to give an example of two-factor authentication and 15 percent of adults did not know where phishing scams occur. Most companies require employees to complete some sort of cyber security training annually, and some of the questions covered in the survey are reviewed in the annual training because these are basic digital skills. Yet, not even half of the surveyed American adults are digitally literate in them. In addition to annual cyber security training, companies should consider providing digital literacy training for their employees that is not tied to a test.

Indicates 42 Million Do Not Have Access."

108 Vogel and Anderson "Americans and Digital Knowledge."

Digital literacy is defined as *"the ability to use information and communication technologies to find, evaluate, create, and communicate information, requiring both cognitive and technical skills."*[109] This is important for several reasons, the least of which is companies that have a digitally literate workforce can contribute toward successful technology adoptions. Moreover, technology and data skills are no longer solely the purview of experts. Accenture's 2019 New Skills Now report states that 85 percent of interviewees believe that the ability to use digital and emerging technologies will remain or become critically important in the next five years and beyond.[110] Giustina Mizzoni from CoderDojo says, *"Digital competence is crucial whether or not you're going to work in technology."* Almost every occupation and business will have a digital component in the future, therefore, it is imperative that every person should have basic digital skills.

A comprehensive list of basic technical skills for entering the *future of work* does not exist, but according to Undercover Recruiter, a global employer branding and talent acquisition blog, lists eight basic skills that everyone should have[111]:

1. social media savviness
2. spreadsheeting
3. presentation skills
4. word processing skills
5. touch typing

---

109 Liana Heitin, "What is Digital Literacy?"

110 Nijma Khan and Tessa Forshaw, "New Skills Now: Inclusion in the Digital Economy."

111 Karim Ansari, "8 Basic Tech Skills Every Employee Should Have."

6. keyboard shortcuts
7. emailing
8. staying with the times.

This blog post is from 2017, and many of the skills listed on it seem rudimentary for a time where workplaces include artificial intelligence and robotics. In an interview with Dr. Terri Horton, a renowned Workforce Futurist, she said that as the *future of work* continues to unfold, most workers are not fluent enough in artificial intelligence, data science, statistics, predictive analytics, and disruptive technologies such as IoT, virtual reality, blockchain, and 3D printing. The demand for these skills and technologies are driven by Industry 4.0 which will continue to shape the future of jobs and work.

> "Anyone, who wants to be employable in the future of work needs to have basic fluency in artificial intelligence and data science, and analytics."
>
> DR. TERRI HORTON, EDD MBA MA, SHRM-CP, PHR, HCS, SWP

Since these skills are not part of the basic curriculum of schools yet, Dr. Horton encourages that parents and teachers look toward online and micro-credential programs and to expose children and themselves to as many experiences as possible with futuristic disruptive technologies. Her advice, while extremely relevant for our youth, is also pertinent for those of us in the middle of our career journeys. What's interesting to note is there is a wide gulf between the eight technical skills listed on the undercover recruiter blog post and those mentioned by Dr. Horton, which further illustrates the need to bridge the digital divide. The technical skills she states as being necessary for the *future of work* are far more advanced than the more rudimentary skills listed in the undercover recruiter blog post. Evidently, there are a lot of technical skills from the basics to current advances to *"staying with the times"* that we need to teach and introduce to the youth to help them become digitally literate.

However, digital literacy extends beyond technical skills; it also requires cognitive skills. Because the Internet has information of every possible kind available, we need to expand reading literacy to include news and media literacy. They need to be able to understand and more importantly evaluate information for its veracity and reliability. As mentioned in chapter four, author Mark Manson writes about how the Internet allows us to gain confirmation bias. In this way the technology and the Internet have not been the *"great equalizer"* that everyone purported them to be, hence the need for the cognitive skills to accompany the digital skills. Media Literacy Now (MLN), the leading national advocacy organization for media literacy education policy in a recent report stated,[112] *"Media literacy is the literacy of the 21st century."*

A recent *New York Times* article described students at Herbert S. Eisenberg, a Coney Island middle school, questioning

---

112 "U.S. Media Literacy Policy Report 2020."

videos on the recent Australian bush fires.[113] They asked questions like *"Who put out the videos?"* and *"What does each source have to gain?"* and so forth. Students at the middle school receive one hour per week of media literacy as part of their English language arts curriculum, for all three years. The MLN 2020 report on US Media Literacy states that without media literacy, there are two attitudes that are adopted about the media consumed.[114] One is confirmation bias as previously written, and the second is a cynicism and disbelief toward everything. Both, attitudes are unfortunate, and do not prepare our youth, which is why digital literacy is important.

Plagiarism, copyright, and ownership are other key topics to teach our youth when discussing media literacy. When I taught at the community college, students had a hard time grasping the notion of ownership of information, especially since so much information is freely available online. They are taught to give credit and provide citations in academic work; however, they need to know that they always need to give credit to other people's ideas, and even though it may be difficult to determine the ownership, every effort should be made to provide such information. For instance, one of the latest trends is a dance sequence called "Renegade" set to the song "Lottery" by Atlanta rapper K-camp.[115] To say that the dance has gone viral is an understatement. People have been doing it in schools and pep rallies across

---

113   Alina Tugend, "These Students are Learning about Fake News and How to Spot It."

114   U.S. Media Literacy Policy Report 2020

115   Taylor Lorenz, "The Original Renegade."

the nation and even celebrities like Lizzo and others have gotten into it. Charli D'Amelio, a TikTok influencer with several million followers, made the dance popular after she posted herself doing the dance on her TikTok. Before she did, it was posted on TikTok in October 2019 by user @ global.jones, but neither one credited Jalaiah Harmon, the creator of the dance.

Harmon, created the dance, and in September 2019, shared it with her followers on Funimate and on her Instagram account. She saw people doing the dance and as it continued to spread across social media, she saw no one giving her credit. She would reach out to the influencers posting the dance via the comments and would ask them to credit her, but no one did. Harmon is not the only person whose ideas have been plagiarized. Other people's dances have been taken from smaller social platforms like Dubsmash, Funimate, Likee, and Triller and posted on TikTok by other influencers who post without giving credit to the originators of the moves. Harmon doesn't bear a grudge against D'Amelio and hopes to collaborate with her in the future; D'Amelio's publicist has shared that she is happy to credit Jalaiah. Teens spend nearly nine hours a day online, outside of school, tweens spend almost six hours a day online, and the majority of their entertainment time online is spent viewing video content.[116]

One of the more recent reactions to the media consumption by youth is to take away the devices in the classrooms. And

---

116 Vicky Rideout, "The Common Sense Census: Media Use by Tweens and Teens."

what I say is *"Let's not take away the devices!"* As adults we all are tethered to our phones and devices and we have to regulate our consumption. How any of us have sat in a meeting and during a lull or a *boring* bit taken out our phone and did some mindless scrolling. We're all guilty of it. The fact of the matter is this is our reality. So why not teach our kids about regulation and proper use? If they're using their phones in the classroom, maybe they're having a moment of cognitive fatigue, or maybe they're not interested.

The solution is not all or nothing. The solutions have to be where technology is used effectively. We can establish firm boundaries on the usage for them and model those ourselves. We can help them figure out what is appropriate and inappropriate. But this tethering to devices is uncharted territory for youth and adults, and instead of trying to get them to behave like *"we did"* in our childhoods, let's help them figure out how to navigate their own.

In early 2020, at the World Economic Forum's Annual Meeting in Davos-Klosters, conversations around the *future of work* suggested that in the next ten years, 50 percent of the jobs will be automated, and the job loss will only be 5 percent, but 90 percent of the jobs will require digital skills.[117] This is a major skills gap that needs to be addressed for particularly vulnerable populations that have no or low technology skills, or do not have reliable access to gain technology skills. While both the President and futurist experts emphasize the need for understanding artificial intelligence

---

117   Robbert van Eerd and Jean Guo, "Jobs will Be Very Different in 10 Years. Here's How to Prepare."

skills and improving technological skills overall, there are still people in the United States who don't have basic technology skills because they cannot afford access to reliable Internet.

We have kids who are being left behind in the Fourth Industrial Revolution, and this is going to impact them economically. Jim Bessen, an economist and lecturer at Boston University, states, *"People who work well with new technologies will see their wages grow; people who do not will be left behind."* Over the last two hundred years, as workers developed relevant skills for the time, technological advancements have been responsible for a tenfold increase in wages.[118] Then we have the youth, who have access to technology but don't know how to use it effectively for the new way of working.

We need to do many things as adults to prepare our children for this new chapter in human industry and history. Some of them are these very basic technological skills that are essential for their success. It's time we thoughtfully reconfigure the way that we teach our children who need to be digitally literate and to be digitally skilled. We need to stop taking away the personal technology entirely from the classrooms because this is their future, and I think we'd all much rather that they know how to effectively use and manage their technology usage as opposed to leaving them to figure things out when they are on their own.

---

118 James Bessen, "How Technology has Affected Wages for the Last 200 Years."

DEVELOPING DIGITAL SKILLS

I have spent the whole book articulating the nine very human skills that we need to teach to our children for the future of work, but I would be remiss if I didn't discuss digital skills. It's hard to say at any point which technology is the one that anyone will need years into the future because things change so quickly. However, we can promote certain skills that will help them be ready for the future.

- Don't assume that digital skills for personal use will translate over to digital skills for professional or academic use. Take time to explain why a specific technological tool is being used and how that can help them in their studies or work. Technology is a tool and we need to teach our children how to best use it. If we can't explain its necessity or importance, then maybe we ought to re-evaluate why we're using it in the first place. Technology shouldn't be incorporated just because it's there and available.

- Digital literacy is very important. It was necessary before but since the 2016 election in the United States, it has become even more imperative that there needs to be a digital literacy component in our education. Social media of all kinds have their own algorithms that display information based on whatever they have gleaned about you through your web usage and through other paid or promotional channels. If we're always looking at information that supports our beliefs, then we won't be able to critically think beyond that. Not to mention that if people are trying to direct you to think one way, you should at least know who is behind the statement. We tell our students Wikipedia is not an academic source and guide them toward journals. We should also spend time analyzing other channels online and help our kids learn how to determine the validity, reliability, and veracity of the information they are consuming.

- Even if your child is not into deeper aspects of computer science, they should have a basic knowledge of coding, data analytics, and an understanding of things like cloud computing, the Internet of Things, artificial intelligence, and machine learning. So many of our products and systems are based upon these, and as I have written, these are the areas that tech will continue to grow, so when it comes to knowing the basics, these are part of it. Staying abreast of trends in technology basics should be a routine part of their lifelong learning.

- It's time once and for all to eliminate the digital divide. Being online and being able to navigate basics online is a fundamental means of survival in this day and age. We need to improve access to broadband for all our citizens. Though this is not a skill to teach to students, it is something they need to be aware of that not everyone has the same access or experience. In the academic or professional world, digital capacity impacts digital capability.

CONCLUSION:

WHAT'S NEXT?

I started writing this book before the pandemic struck. As I wrote earlier, I have been thinking about my kids' careers for a long time. My husband and I come from a culture, where while we were growing up our parents' generation pushed our generation to become either doctors or engineers; especially male children. So, we knew that we would not be forcing any choices upon our kids. At first our kids followed the same path as most young children of various things that they thought were cool, but it was the *"youtuber"* choice that really had an impact on us. At first, we dismissed it as a fleeting fancy, like all the others. But it stuck around for a while, and it forced my husband and me to confront our own conditioning of how life plays out, which was high school, followed by college, and then a career.

But more than the start of the journey for the book, the pandemic has illustrated how much our old paradigms need to change. If the urgency wasn't there before, it's there now because of the immediate impact and the long-term effects that this will have on education. First, nationwide we have had our kids out of school for anywhere from eight to twelve weeks of the academic year, and as of now we don't know what will happen in the fall. Transitioning to distance learning was difficult for our school district and for many others. Homeschooling is just another layer of complication in an already fractured situation. Though all children will be impacted by all these added complications, those who will feel the effects most long-term, and those who are already at a disadvantage because the pandemic has brought inequities across all levels to the forefront.

Students from disadvantaged backgrounds who were on equal footing with their peers on college campuses are feeling the difference when they're back home. They may have shelter or food insecurity. They also may not have access to reliable technology. Similarly, there are kids in the Kindergarten through twelfth grade system who depend on the meals at school and who don't have parents that can engage in the curriculum or have the technology they need. Paul Reville, former secretary of education in Massachusetts, shares in an interview with *The Harvard Gazette*, that this is the first time *"the general public have become more aware than at any time in my memory of the inequities in children's lives outside of school.*[119] *Suddenly we see front-page coverage about food deficits, inadequate access to health and mental health, problems with housing stability, and access to educational technology and internet."* Educators have known and had to deal with these issues as routine, but as Reville shares, this is the first time that society as a whole is being exposed to the disparities that the education system has to contend with.

---

119 Liz Mineo, "Time to Fix American Education with Race-For-Space Resolve."

The impact that this piece-meal education will have on this generation of kids is still unknown, but the pandemic has thrust upon us an opportunity to rethink the way we educate our children. As opposed to holding onto old paradigms, we should look at this as an opportunity to begin making changes that will help bring our education system more in line with what our youth needs. Because the pandemic has brought to light the myriad factors that impact our youth and their education, Sir Ken Robinson's words *"educate the whole child"* have never held truer; especially as we are entering the Fourth Industrial Revolution, a time that *"is fundamentally changing the way we live, work, and relate to one another."*[120] And as we are being ushered into that era, we are also facing a global crisis unlike what any of us have witnessed in our lives.

So, what's next?

First, the book identifies key skills our youth should develop to adapt and survive in a new economy with non-linear career paths. While the pandemic is not the reason behind the need for human skills, it has highlighted them with bright neon signs. We have used these skills relating to ourselves and others far more than any other technological or such skill. Moving forward there has to be a stronger case for incorporating these skills into our schools' character and citizenship goals in addition to utilizing the curriculum to build them because our kids will need them. We hope they won't face pandemics, but they will face crises

---

120 Schwab, "The Fourth Industrial Revolution: What It Means and How to Respond."

of large scale whether it is in a particular company, industry, or globally and when everything else goes down, the people who come out on top are the people who are good at being human.

Second, in addition to soft skills, there is also a greater need for education and business to align workforce readiness related goals. Because, *"on the one hand, when teachers know which soft skills they should be emphasizing, they are able to make simple, effective changes. Many K-12 educators, however, lack the flexibility, resources, and support to bridge the soft skills gap on their own and require help from credible partners. On the other hand, nobody knows better which skills employers are looking for than businesses themselves. Unfortunately, the current approach of waiting to bridge an employee's skills gap "on the job" is too expensive and comes too late. To create a reliable talent pipeline, businesses have to work hand-in-hand with schools."*[121]

Third, and final, we ALL need to develop a lifelong learning mindset. Lifelong learning is essential to updating all our skills, regardless of whether they are our human skills or professional skills. Children are born with an innate curiosity to figure out how the world works and learn how to do things. We rush to get them into pre-schools and schools, where the innate curiosity is replaced by prescribed curriculum standards. What we need to remember is that academics is a means to an end and not the actual end and by pushing a standardized expectation, we kill the curiosity to learn that we are born with.

---

121 Bridging the Soft Skills Gap, 2017.

HUMAN SKILLS

"Work is changing. Not just the creation of new types of jobs, but also the way work is conducted. The speed of change also calls for an updated skillset, calling for workers to quickly adapt, to learn new approaches to challenges, to think more critically, and to collaborate with people they may never meet face to face."[122]

ROBERTA SAWATZKY MA, CPHR, SHRM-SCP

SCHOOL OF BUSINESS, OKANAGAN COLLEGE

There are plenty of white papers and articles by the world's top workforce management consulting firms and business leaders about the *future of work* being human. Even this book is all about the human skills. The soft skills that make us uniquely human cannot be replaced or replicated. So, the worry that in the *future of work* we will be replaced by machines is unfounded.

There will be robots that we will work alongside. They will do the work that is *"dull, dirty, or dangerous"* or all the above. By using robots, humans will have the opportunity to do more

---

122 Laurel Farrer, "Future of Education and Future of Work—Do They Match?"

meaningful work. For example, one way that some experts can see this happening is in hospitals. They might use robots to do routine checks, like checking patients' blood pressure, temperature, heart rate, dispense medication, thus, leaving nurses to handle distress calls or evaluating changing symptoms; while leaving nurses and doctors to focus on those situations that require a judgment call or provide additional comfort to the patient.

Conversely, when it comes to artificial intelligence, humans may be involved in helping machines learn. Because of the speed of evolving technology and the fact that for certain specialized functions, machines will be instantly better than humans. It is likely that our young people will be teaching machines the jobs that they have, while re-skilling for their next job. Some jobs will be taken over by artificial intelligence when it has learned enough, but some of the jobs will be augmented by artificial intelligence, and people will work in tandem with them. This will leave people an opportunity to do more of the meaningful and inspiring work than the rote work that humans have been doing for a while.

"Preparing students for tomorrow's jobs requires breaking down the silos within education."[123]

STEPHANE KASRIEL WORLD ECONOMIC FORUM

Our education system is still largely the same as it was when it started in the early twentieth century. We still group students together by age. We continue to promote order and obedience over creativity. Standardized testing is rampant across the school system. Academics are taught separately. Classrooms are overcrowded. American high school students consistently underperform compared to students in other countries[124]... the list goes on. Moreover, the skills gap has illustrated that *"traditional education and career pathways weren't designed to develop skills for a fast-changing market or to match the speed of changing industry requirements."*[125] Our old models do not work well in the new world, and we need to move away from our traditional model of school followed by college. It's a template that no longer works for us and will not work for our youth.

---

123 Stephane Kasriel, "4 Predictions for the Future of Work."

124 "OECD Il.ibrary | PISA 2018 Results (Volume I): What Students Know and Can Do" 2020.

125 Cheryl Oldham, "The Evolution of the Skills Gap Requires 21st Century Solutions."

Tom Vander Ark, a LinkedIn Top Voice in Education and CEO of Getting Smart, says that *"Learning for the twenty-first century is both personal and personalized, and combines learner voice and choice with thoughtful guidance to shape learning journeys."* He also recommends four ways to help young people develop the skills they need for now and as adults.[126] First is to integrate more *"community-connected"* projects. Second is to provide more opportunities to serve and take on leadership roles. The third is to have more work-based learning that includes job shadows, client projects, and internships. Finally, Vander Ark recommends that the youth be given more guidance in learning journeys. Similarly, Merrilea Mayo, COO of Social Tech believes that with the workplace demanding a different skill set than the ones traditionally learned in school and with increasingly higher education costs being what they are, the *future of work* will be more of an *"integration of working and learning."* Mayo sees a continuous cycle of layered working and learning being the end point of higher education in the next decade.

Colleges are already re-examining ways to meet the needs of the students and the workforce. For instance, the University System of Georgia is creating *"nexus"* degrees, which are two-year degrees *"that require students to take internships and upper-division courses–demands typically not found in associate degrees."*[127] Some other colleges, especially community colleges, are strengthening pathways to four-year schools so students don't lose out on credits and can earn a bachelor's

---

126 Tom Vander Ark, "What is 21st Century Learning? How do we get More?"
127 Mikhail Zinshteyn, "How the Skills Gap is Changing the Degree Path."

degree at a lower cost. While these are good solutions for establishing a better path from college to the workforce, the human skills that we need aren't learned during a four-year degree. These are lifelong skills, and they need to be developed over a longer period.

When I was teaching, I would sometimes have old students email me or come visit me. The thing that I was thanked for the most or that they remembered the most from my classroom was the diversity of content I had them read. Each of them had some sort of anecdote to share about something they read in my class that they didn't think was relevant to them, but in a later experience they found it to be useful. I had, over the course of my teaching, taken to a thematic cross curriculum approach to what we would read. For instance, in one advanced reading course we would read *The Hunger Games* as the long form reading choice and in addition to the novel the students would also read articles related to the themes of poverty, income inequality, the lure of reality TV, totalitarian regimes, and scientific advances. I would try to find reading material in the topics that related to the fields that the students were pursuing or try to make connections across what they were learning in some of their other courses. Whether it was that they were able to converse with someone or that it helped them think of things in an interconnected way, these students recognized the value, to an extent, of a more interdisciplinary and diverse educational experience—a breakdown of those academic silos.

In addition to having a more interdisciplinary approach toward the curriculum, we also need to rethink how we group students, and the demands that we place on them to be well behaved in the classroom, not to mention the spaces themselves. However, these issues are much larger and systemic, and institutional behavior can be hard to change. As I mentioned, while part of me wants to blow up the current model and build a new one from scratch that is not a possibility.

LIFELONG LEARNING

"Skill. Re-skill. Up-skill. Repeat."

This is the mantra we need to adopt for the *future of work* for all of us because we will all need to frequently update our skills. In fact, we may be re-skilling while at one job in preparation for another job. Stephane Kasriel, CEO of Upwork, writes in the World Economic Forum, that *"the half-life of professional skills was once estimated at ten to fifteen years, meaning that the value of those skills would decline by half–or half the knowledge associated with the skills would become irrelevant–in a decade or so. Today, the half-life of a learned skill is estimated to be five years and even shorter for technical skills, meaning a skill learned today will be about half as valuable in just five years or less."*[128] With the rapid pace of development in the workforce, college curriculums cannot keep pace with technology and other workforce advancements, so adapting a mindset of lifelong learning is no longer for the curious—students-at-heart—kind of people.

---

128 Stephane Kasriel, "Skill, re-skill and re-skill again. How to keep up with the future of work."

Some people are naturally curious and seek out learning opportunities. Kids illustrate this best when they are young, and they want to learn and do everything themselves. As the adults in their lives, we need to retrain our brains to maintain this innate curiosity, and we need to enable, encourage, and provide our youth the opportunities to seek and learn about things that are interesting to them because over time, whether it's through school or through over-scheduling with various activities, children tend to lose their curiosity, and as they become adults they settle into a fixed mindset.

As I wrote earlier the Korn Ferry Hay Group research found that human capital holds the greatest value for organizations now and in the future, in spite of the emphasis on technology in the future of work.[129] *"People, labor, knowledge—will be worth as much as $1.2 quadrillion over the next five years. In contrast, physical capital—inventory, real estate, and technology—will be worth an estimated $521 trillion. Human talent and intelligence are 2.33 times more valuable than everything else put together."*[130] Paul Reville says that *"within this coronavirus crisis there is an opportunity to reshape American education.*[131] *The only precedent in our field was when the Sputnik went up in 1957, and suddenly, Americans became very worried that their educational system wasn't competitive with that of the Soviet Union...And we decided to dramatically boost the involvement of the federal government in schooling... we decided to look at education as an important factor in human capital development in this country."*

---

129 Distefano, et al., "The Trillion-Dollar Difference."

130 Kane, et al., "The Very Human Future of Work."

131 Mineo, "Time to Fix American Education with Race-For-Space Resolve."

We're at a similar precipice to fundamentally alter our educational system and this time it's not about reaching new heights out of this world, but about reaching new heights within this world.

APPENDIX

INTRODUCTION

Østergaard, Simon Fuglsang, and Adam Graafland Nordlund. "The 4 Biggest Challenges to Our Higher Education Model—and What to Do about Them." *World Economic Forum*, December 20, 2019. https://www.weforum.org/agenda/2019/12/fourth-industrial-revolution-higher-education-challenges/.

Schwab, Klaus. "The Fourth Industrial Revolution: What It Means and How to Respond." *World Economic Forum*, January 14, 2016. https://www.weforum.org/agenda/2016/01/the-fourth-industrial-revolution-what-it-means-and-how-to-respond/.

Toffler, Alvin. *Oxford Essential Quotations 4th ed*, ed. Susan Ratcliffe. Oxford University Press, 2016. https://www.oxfordreference.com/view/10.1093/acref/9780191826719.001.0001/q-oro-ed4-00010964/.

CHAPTER 1

Armstrong, Katie, Michele Parmelee, Stasha Santifort, Jamira Burley, Justin W. van Fleet, Maggie Koziol, Rebecca Greenberg, Jeff Schwartz and Renee Tetrick. "Preparing Tomorrow's Workforce for the Fourth Industrial Revolution. For business: A framework for action." *Deloitte Global and The Global Business Coalition for Education*, September 2018. https://www2.deloitte.com/content/dam/Deloitte/global/Documents/About-Deloitte/gx-preparing-tomorrow-workforce-for-4IR.pdf/.

Bond, Tyler. "What Happened To Private Sector Pensions?" National Public Pension Coalition. August 4, 2016. https://protectpensions.org/2016/08/04/happened-private-sector-pensions/.

Bridging The Soft Skills Gap. *U.S. Chamber of Commerce Foundation*. November 6, 2017. https://www.uschamberfoundation.org/reports/soft-skills-gap/.

"Future of Work" *Deloitte United States*. Accessed October 11, 2019. https://www2.deloitte.com/us/en/insights/focus/technology-and-the-future-of-work.html/.

Hinton, Sean. "How The Fourth Industrial Revolution Is Impacting The Future of Work." *Forbes*, October 19, 2019. https://www.forbes.com/sites/theyec/2018/10/19/how-the-fourth-industrial-revolution-is-impacting-the-future-of-work/#2766411265a7/.

Marr, Bernard. "What is Industry 4.0? Here's A Super Easy Explanation For Anyone." *Forbes*, September 2, 2018. https://www.forbes.com/sites/bernardmarr/2018/09/02/what-is-industry-4-0-heres-a-super-easy-explanation-for-anyone/#1cd379279788/.

Menon, Jayant. "Why the Fourth Industrial Revolution Could Spell More Jobs—Not Fewer." *World Economic Forum,* September 17, 2019. https://www.weforum.org/agenda/2019/09/fourth-industrial-revolution-jobs/.

Østergaard, Simon Fuglsang and Adam Graafland Nordlund. "The 4 Biggest Challenges to Our Higher Education Model—and What to Do About Them." *World Economic Forum,* December 20, 2019. https://www.weforum.org/agenda/2019/12/fourth-industrial-revolution-higher-education-challenges/.

Rosenberg, Marc. "The Coming Knowledge Tsunami." *Marc My Words* (blog). *Learning Solutions.* October 10, 2017. https://learningsolutionsmag.com/articles/2468/marc-my-words-the-coming-knowledge-tsunami/.

Society for Human Resource Management. "The Skills Gap 2019." *SHRM,* February 5, 2019. https://www.shrm.org/hr-today/trends-and-forecasting/research-and-surveys/pages/skills-gap-2019.aspx/.

Toews, Rob. "What Does 'Artificial Intelligence' Really Mean?" *Forbes,* February 17, 2020. https://www.forbes.com/sites/robtoews/2020/02/17/what-does-artificial-intelligence-really-mean/#-3573d2a4c5f6/.

Tyagarajan, Tiger. "To Prepare for Automation, Stay Curious and Don't Stop Learning." *Harvard Business Review.* October 8, 2019. https://hbr.org/2019/10/to-prepare-for-automation-stay-curious-and-dont-stop-learning/.

Volini, Erica, Jeff Schwartz, Indranil Roy, Maren Hauptmann, Yves Van Durme, Brad Denny, and Josh Bersin. "From Jobs to Superjobs." *Deloitte Insights.* April 11, 2019. https://www2.deloitte.com/us/en/insights/focus/human-capital-trends/2019/impact-of-ai-turning-jobs-into-superjobs.html#/.

PART II

CHAPTER 2

Goleman, Daniel. *Working with Emotional Intelligence.* New York City: Bantam, 1998.

Haslam, Nick. "What's the Difference Between Traumatic Fear and Moral Anger? Trigger Warnings Won't Tell You." *The Conversation.* May 8, 2017. https://theconversation.com/whats-the-difference-between-traumatic-fear-and-moral-anger-trigger-warnings-wont-tell-you-77365/.

Morin, Amanda. "The Importance of Self-Awareness in Kids." *Understood.Org.* Accessed April 9, 2020. https://www.understood.org/en/friends-feelings/empowering-your-child/self-awareness/the-importance-of-self-awareness/.

CHAPTER 3

"Emotional and Social Intelligence Leadership Competencies: An Overview." *Key Step Media.* April 11, 2017. https://www.keystepmedia.com/emotional-social-intelligence-leadership-competencies/.

Goleman, Daniel. "Balance Your Need to Achieve." *Korn Ferry*. Accessed January 11, 2020. https://www.kornferry.com/insights/articles/achievement-orientation/.

Kanter, Rosabeth Moss. "Surprises Are the New Normal; Resilience Is the New Skill." *Harvard Business Review*. July 17, 2013. https://hbr.org/2013/07/surprises-are-the-new-normal-r/.

Marano, Hara Estroff. "Our Brain's Negative Bias." *Psychology Today*. June 20, 2003. https://www.psychologytoday.com/us/articles/200306/our-brains-negative-bias/.

Ovans, Andrea. "What Resilience Means, and Why It Matters." *Harvard Business Review*. January 5, 2015. https://hbr.org/2015/01/what-resilience-means-and-why-it-matters/.

Palmiter, David, Mary Alvord, Rosalind Dorlen, Lillian Comas-Diaz, Suniya S. Luthar, Salvatore R. Maddi, H. Katherine (Kit) O'Neill, Karen W. Saakvitne, and Richard G Tedeschi. "Building Your Resilience." *American Psychological Association*. February 1, 2020. https://www.apa.org/topics/resilience/.

"Reskilling Revolution Program." *World Economic Forum*. Accessed April 9, 2020. https://www.weforum.org/projects/reskilling-revolution-platform/.

Waverman, Emma. "Snowplow Parenting: What to Know About the Controversial Technique." *Today's Parent*. March 22, 2019. https://www.todaysparent.com/blogs/snowplow-parenting-the-latest-controversial-technique/.

CHAPTER 4

Beck, Kent, Mike Beedle, Arie van Bennekum, Alistair Cockburn, Ward Cunningham, Martin Fowler, James Grenning et al. "Manifesto for Agile Software Development." *agilemanifesto.org.* Accessed February 18, 2020. http://agilemanifesto.org/.

Istrate, Emilia and Jonathan Harris. "The Future of Work: The Rise of the Gig Economy." *National Association of Counties.* November 2017. https://www.naco.org/featured-resources/future-work-rise-gig-economy/.

Mahdawi, Arwa. "What Jobs Will Still Be Around in 20 Years? Read This to Prepare Your Future." *The Guardian.* June 26, 2017. https://www.theguardian.com/us-news/2017/jun/26/jobs-future-automation-robots-skills-creative-health/.

Manyika, James, Susan Lund, Jacques Bughin, Kelsey Robinson, Jan Mischke, and Deepa Mahajan. "Independent Work: Choice, Necessity, and the Gig Economy." *McKinsey Global Institute.* October 10, 2016. https://www.mckinsey.com/featured-insights/employment-and-growth/independent-work-choice-necessity-and-the-gig-economy/.

Muhammed, Abdullahi. "Busting the Gig Economy Myths: 40% of Gig Workers Now Earn Six-Figures Per Year." *Forbes.* June 1, 2019. https://www.forbes.com/sites/abdullahimuhammed/2019/06/01/busting-the-gig-economy-myths-40-of-gig-workers-now-earn-six-figures-per-year/#7601e7f74542/.

Mulcahy, Diane. "Universities Should Be Preparing Students For The Gig Economy." *Harvard Business Review.* October 3, 2019.

https://hbr.org/2019/10/universities-should-be-preparing-students-for-the-gig-economy/.

Simovic, Dragomir. "The Ultimate List of Remote Work Statistics—2020 Edition." *Smallbizgenius*. October 28, 2019. https://www.smallbizgenius.net/by-the-numbers/remote-work-statistics/#gref/.

Varhol, Peter. "To Agility and Beyond: The History—and Legacy—of Agile Development." *Tech Beacon*. Accessed Feb 18, 2020. https://techbeacon.com/app-dev-testing/agility-beyond-history-legacy-agile-development/.

Wakabayashi, Daisuke. "Google's Shadow Work Force: Temps Who Outnumber Full-Time Employees." *The New York Times*. May 28, 2019. https://www.nytimes.com/2019/05/28/technology/google-temp-workers.html/.

CHAPTER 5

Godin, Seth. *Stop Stealing Dreams: What is School For? Seths.Blog*. September 2, 2014. https://seths.blog/wp-content/uploads/2014/09/stopstealingdreams-screen-2015.pdf/.

Kahneman, Daniel. *Thinking Fast and Slow*. New York: Farrar, Straus and Geroux, 2011.

Leonhardt, Megan. "Nigerian Prince Email Scams Still Rake in Over $700,000 a year—Here's How To Protect Yourself." *CNBC*. April 18, 2019. https://www.cnbc.com/2019/04/18/nigerian-prince-scams-still-rake-in-over-700000-dollars-a-year.html/.

Manson, Mark. *The World is Fucked and I'm Pretty Sure It's the Internet's Fault. MarkManson*. Accessed February 19, 2020. https://markmanson.net/the-world-is-fucked/.

"OECD Ilibrary | PISA 2018 Results (Volume I): What Students Know and Can Do." 2020. *Oecd-Ilibrary.Org*. https://www.oecd-ilibrary.org/education/pisa-2018-results-volume-i_5f07c754-en/.

"OECD Ilibrary | PISA 2018 Results (Volume III): What School Life Means for Students' LIves." 2020. *Oecd-Ilibrary.Org*. https://www.oecd-ilibrary.org/education/pisa-2018-results-volume-iii_acd78851-en/.

CHAPTER 6

Berger, Larry. "What Do Young People Need to Learn Today to Be Prepared For Tomorrow?" *XQsuperschool (Blog)*. July 9, 2019. https://xqsuperschool.org/blog/teaching-strategies/prepared-for-tomorrow/.

Cascone, Sarah. "Maurizio Cattelan Is Taping Bananas to a Wall at Art Basel Miami Beach and Selling Them for $120,000 Each." *Artnet News*. December 4, 2019. https://news.artnet.com/market/maurizio-cattelan-banana-art-basel-miami-beach-1722516/.

Free, Cathy. "Portraits on Campus Lacked Diversity, So this Artist Painted the Blue-collar Workers Who 'Really Run Things'." *The Washington Post*. January 24, 2020. https://www.washingtonpost.com/lifestyle/2020/01/24/portraits-campus-lacked-diversity-so-this-artist-painted-blue-collar-workers-who-really-run-things/.

Goodman, Stacey. "Fuel Creativity in the Classroom With Divergent Thinking." *Edutopia.* March 18, 2014. https://www.edutopia.org/blog/fueling-creativity-through-divergent-thinking-classroom-stacey-goodman/.

Gray, Alex. "The 10 Skills You Need To Thrive In The Fourth Industrial Revolution." *World Economic Forum.* January 19, 2016. https://www.weforum.org/agenda/2016/01/the-10-skills-you-need-to-thrive-in-the-fourth-industrial-revolution/.

Kim, Daniel H. "Introduction to Systems Thinking." *The Systems Thinker.* Accessed January 12, 2020. https://thesystemsthinker.com/wp-content/uploads/2016/03/Introduction-to-Systems-Thinking-IMS013Epk.pdf/.

Leon, Adam. "3 Great Examples of Design Thinking in Action." *Medium.* June 26, 2016. https://medium.com/swlh/3-great-examples-of-design-thinking-in-action-a96461538c4a/.

Power, Rhett. "Give Divergent Thinking a Chance to Solve Your Biggest Challenges." *Inc.* December 26, 2019. https://www.inc.com/rhett-power/give-divergent-thinking-a-chance-to-solve-your-biggest-challenges.html/.

Robinson, Sir Ken. "Do Schools Kill Creativity?" Filmed February 2006 at a TED Conference, TED video, 19:13. https://www.ted.com/talks/sir_ken_robinson_do_schools_kill_creativity/.

Weiss, C.C. "Ford's New Kick-Activated Tailgate Provides Hands-Free Opening." *Newatlas.* March 7, 2012. https://newatlas.com/ford-kick-activated-tailgate/21746/.

PART III

Distefano, Michael, Alan Guarino, Jeanne MacDonald, Stuart S. Crandell, and Jean-Marc Lauchez. "The Trillion-Dollar Difference." *Korn Ferry*. Accessed March 9, 2020. https://www.kornferry.com/insights/articles/the-trillion-dollar-difference?all-topics/.

Kane, Karen, Russell Pearlman, and Hazel Euan-Smith. "The Very Human Future of Work." *Korn Ferry*. Accessed March 9, 2020. https://www.kornferry.com/insights/articles/2030-the-very-human-future-of-work/.

CHAPTER 7

Beck, M and Barry Libert. "The Rise of AI Makes Emotional Intelligence More Important." *Harvard Business Review*. February 15, 2017. https://hbr.org/2017/02/the-rise-of-ai-makes-emotional-intelligence-more-important/.

Besinger, Greg. "The Web's Most Maniacal Bargain Hunters." *The Wall Street Journal*. April 9, 2015. https://www.wsj.com/articles/webs-most-maniacal-bargain-hunters-1428619524.

Delgado, Maria. "The Path to Prosperity: Why the Future of Work is Human." *Deloitte (Blog)*. September 16, 2019. https://www2.deloitte.com/au/en/blog/diversity-inclusion-blog/2019/path-to-prosperity-why-future-of-work-is-human.html#/.

Lee, Bruce. "Cigna Finds More Evidence of Loneliness In America." *Forbes*. May 1, 2018. https://www.forbes.com/sites/brucelee/2018/05/01/here-is-more-evidence-that-americans-are-lonely-and-what-should-be-done/.

Matthews, Dona. "Empathy: Where Kindness, Compassion, and Happiness Begin." *Psychology Today*. October 31, 2019. https://www.psychologytoday.com/us/blog/going-beyond-intelligence/201910/empathy-where-kindness-compassion-and-happiness-begin/.

Nicas, Jack. "He Has 17,700 Bottles of Hand Sanitizer and Nowhere to Sell Them." *The New York Times*. March 14, 2020. https://www.nytimes.com/2020/03/14/technology/coronavirus-purell-wipes-amazon-sellers.html/.

CHAPTER 8

Chappell, Bill. "For $450, This Japanese Company Will Quit Your Job for You." *NPR*. August 28, 2018. https://www.npr.org/2018/08/28/642597968/for-450-this-japanese-company-will-quit-your-job-for-you.

Dashman, Lydia. "The Latest Trend for Job Seekers: Ghosting Employers." *FastCompany*. August 26, 2019. https://www.fastcompany.com/90395341/83-of-employers-say-job-seekers-have-ghosted-them/.

Hagel, John, John Selly Brown, and Maggie Wooll. "Skills Change, But Capabilities Endure." *Deloitte Insights*. August 30, 2019. https://www2.deloitte.com/us/en/insights/focus/technology-and-the-future-of-work/future-of-work-human-capabilities.html/.

Hess, Abigail. "Here's How Many Hours American Workers Spend On Email Each Day." *CNBC*. September 22, 2019. https://www.cnbc.com/2019/09/22/heres-how-many-hours-american-workers-spend-on-email-each-day.html/.

Moore, Kaleigh. "Study: 73% of Employers Want Candidates With This Skill." *Inc.* April 7, 2016. https://www.inc.com/kaleigh-moore/study-73-of-employers-want-candidates-with-this-skill.html/.

Sullivan, Emily. "In A Hot Labor Market, Some Employees Are 'Ghosting' Bad Bosses." *NPR.* January 25, 2019. https://www.npr.org/2019/01/25/688303552/in-a-hot-labor-market-some-employees-are-ghosting-on-bad-bosses/.

CHAPTER 9

Back, Jamie. "Teaching Students How to Work Together." *Getting Smart.* January 13, 2018. https://www.gettingsmart.com/2018/01/teaching-students-how-to-work-together/.

Cooke, Nancy. "5 Ways to Help Robots Work Together With People." *The Conversation.* November 28, 2018. https://theconversation.com/5-ways-to-help-robots-work-together-with-people-101419.

Cooke, Nancy. "Your Next Colleague Could Be A Robot. Here's How to Get Along." *Fast Company.* November 29, 2018. https://www.fastcompany.com/90273477/your-next-colleague-could-be-a-robot-heres-how-to-get-along/.

Duhigg, Charles. "What Google Learned from Its Quest to Build the Perfect Team." *The New York Times.* February 25, 2016. https://www.nytimes.com/2016/02/28/magazine/what-google-learned-from-its-quest-to-build-the-perfect-team.html/.

Guizzo, Erico. "What Is A Robot?" *Robots, Institute of Electrical and Electronics Engineers.* Accessed, March 24, 2020. https://robots.ieee.org/learn/.

Hickman, Adam and Jennifer Robison. "Is Working Remotely Effective? Gallup Research Says Yes." *Gallup.* January 24, 2020. https://www.gallup.com/workplace/283985/working-remotely-effective-gallup-research-says-yes.aspx/.

Kaplan, Elle. "Google Found the Most Successful Teams Share These 5 Traits." *CNBC.* July 16, 2018. https://www.cnbc.com/2018/07/16/the-5-traits-of-the-most-successful-teams-according-to-google.html/.

Messersmith, Amber S. "Preparing Students for 21st Century Teamwork: Effective Collaboration in the Online Group Communication Course." *Communication Teacher,* 29 no.4 (2015): 219-226, DOI: 10.1080/17404622.2015.1046188/.

Prichard, Jane. S, Lewis A. Bizo and Robert J. Stratford. "The Educational Impact of Team-Skills Training: Preparing Students to Work in Groups." *British Journal of Education Psychology,* 76 (2006):119-140.

Redwood, Stephen, Mark Holmstrom, and Zach Vetter. "Transitioning to the Future of Work and the Workplace." *Deloitte Global.* September 2016. https://www2.deloitte.com/content/dam/Deloitte/us/Documents/human-capital/us-human-capital-transitioning-to-the-future-of-work.pdf/.

Ryan, Major General Mick. "How to Plan for the Coming Era of Human-Machine Teaming." *Defense One.* April 25, 2018. https://www.defenseone.com/ideas/2018/04/how-plan-coming-era-human-machine-teaming/147718/.

Siebdrat, Frank, Martin Hoegl, and Holger Ernst. "How to Manage Virtual Teams." *MIT Sloan Management Review.* July 1, 2009. https://sloanreview.mit.edu/article/how-to-manage-virtual-teams/.

"The Workplace of the Future." *Wired Brand Lab.* Accessed May 7, 2020. https://www.wired.com/brandlab/2018/06/the-workplace-of-the-future/.

Welker, Martin. "The Future of Productivity: Teamwork and Collaboration." *Entrepreneur.* July 27, 2017. https://www.entrepreneur.com/article/295265/.

CHAPTER 10

Barth, F. Diane. "Are You Conflict Avoidant Or Conflict Seeking?" *Psychology Today.* October 1, 2017. https://www.psychologytoday.com/us/blog/the-couch/201710/are-you-conflict-avoidant-or-conflict-seeking/.

Chun, Rene. "A Shocking Number of Killers Murder Their Co-workers." *The Atlantic.* October 2018. https://www.theatlantic.com/magazine/archive/2018/10/the-killer-in-the-cubicle/568303/.

"Developing Personal Accountability." *MindTools.* Accessed November 17, 2019.

Doucette, Mitchell, Maria.T.Bulzacchelli, , Shannon Frattaroli, and Cassandra K. Crifasi. "Workplace homicides committed by firearm: recent trends and narrative text analysis." *Injury Epidemiology.* 6, 5 (2019). https://doi.org/10.1186/s40621-019-0184-0

Gallo, Amy. *Dealing with Conflict*. Boston: Harvard Business School Publishing Corporation, 2017.

Green, Alison. "Two of My Employees won't Speak to Each Other." *Ask A Manager (Blog)*. November 19, 2019. https://www.askamanager.org/2019/11/two-of-my-employees-wont-speak-to-each-other.html/.

Raymond, Jonathan. "Do You Understand What Accountability Really Means?" *Harvard Business Review*. October 13, 2016. https://hbr.org/2016/10/do-you-understand-what-accountability-really-means/.

Simon, Darran. "Virginia Beach Gunman's Resignation Email Hours Before Mass Shooting Offers No Clues." *CNN*. June 3, 2019. https://www.cnn.com/2019/06/03/us/virginia-beach-shooter-resignation-letter/index.html/.

"U.S. Mass Killings Hit A Record High In 2019: 'This Seems to be the Age of Mass Shootings.'" *USA Today*. December 28, 2019. https://www.usatoday.com/story/news/nation/2019/12/28/us-mass-shootings-killings-2019-41-record-high/2748794001/.

"Workplace Conflict and How Businesses can Harness it to Thrive." *CPP Global Human Capital Report*. July, 2008.

"Workplace Homicides in 2017." 2019. *Bls.Gov*. https://www.bls.gov/iif/oshwc/cfoi/workplace-homicides-2017.htm.

"Your Best Employees Are Leaving. But is it Personal or Practical?" *Randstad US*. August 28, 2018. https://rlc.randstadusa.com/press-room/press-releases/your-best-employees-are-leaving-but-is-it-personal-or-practical/.

CHAPTER 11

Ansari, Karim. "8 Basic Tech Skills Every Employee Should Have." *Undercover Recruiter (blog)*. Accessed February 20, 2020. https://theundercoverrecruiter.com/8-tech-skills/.

Bessen, James. "How Technology Has Affected Wages For The Last 200 Years." *Harvard Business Review*. April 29, 2015. https://hbr.org/2015/04/how-technology-has-affected-wages-for-the-last-200-years/.

Busby, John, Julia Tanberk, and BroadbandNow Team. "FCC Reports Broadband Unavailable to 21.3 Million Americans, BroadbandNow Study Indicates 42 Million Do Not Have Access." February 3, 2020. https://broadbandnow.com/research/fcc-under-estimates-unserved-by-50-percent/.

Duarte, Carrie, Dan Staley, and Bhushan Sethi. "Our Status with Tech at Work: It's Complicated." October, 2018. https://www.pwc.com/us/en/services/consulting/library/images/PwC_CIS-Tech-at-Work.pdf/.

"Executive Order on Maintaining American Leadership in Artificial Intelligence | The White House" *The White House*. February 11, 2019. https://www.whitehouse.gov/presidential-actions/executive-order-maintaining-american-leadership-artificial-intelligence/.

Federal Communication Commission, "2019 Broadband Deployment Report." May 29, 2019. https://www.fcc.gov/reports-research/reports/broadband-progress-reports/2019-broadband-deployment-report/.

Heitin, Liana. "What is Digital Literacy?" *Education Week.* November 8, 2016. https://www.edweek.org/ew/articles/2016/11/09/what-is-digital-literacy.html/.

Khan, Nijma and Tessa Forshaw. "New Skills Now: Inclusion in the Digital Economy." Accessed March 12, 2020. https://www.accenture.com/_acnmedia/pdf-63/accenture-new-skills-now-inclusion-in-the-digital.pdf/.

Lorenz, Taylor. "The Original Renegade." *The New York Times.* February 18, 2020. https://www.nytimes.com/2020/02/13/style/the-original-renegade.html/.

Rideout, Vicky. "The Common Sense Census: Media Use by Tweens and Teens." *Common Sense Media.* Accessed February 19, 2020. https://www.commonsensemedia.org/sites/default/files/uploads/research/census_executivesummary.pdf/.

Steele, Carmen. "What is the Digital Divide?" February 22, 2019. http://www.digitaldividecouncil.com/what-is-the-digital-divide/.

Tugend, Alina. "These Students are Learning about Fake News and How to Spot It." *The New York Times.* February 20, 2020. https://www.nytimes.com/2020/02/20/education/learning/news-literacy-2016-election.html.

"U.S. Media Literacy Policy Report 2020." January 2020. https://medialiteracynow.org/wp-content/uploads/2020/01/U.S.-Media-Literacy-Policy-Report-2020.pdf/.

Van Eerd, Robbert and Jean Guo. "Jobs will be Very Different in 10 Years. Here's How to Prepare." *World Economic Forum.* January 17, 2020. https://www.weforum.org/agenda/2020/01/future-of-work/.

Vogels, Emily A. and Monica Anderson. "Americans and Digital Knowledge." *Pew Research Center.* October 9, 2019. https://www.pewresearch.org/internet/2019/10/09/americans-and-digital-knowledge/.

"What Is Slack?" Accessed April 1, 2020. https://slack.com/help/articles/115004071768-What-is-Slack-/.

CONCLUSION

Bridging the Soft Skills Gap. *U.S. Chamber of Commerce Foundation.* November 6, 2017. https://www.uschamberfoundation.org/reports/soft-skills-gap/.

Distefano, Michael, Alan Guarino, Jeanne MacDonald, Stuart S. Crandell, and Jean-Marc Lauchez. "The Trillion-Dollar Difference." *Korn Ferry.* Accessed March 9, 2020. https://www.kornferry.com/insights/articles/the-trillion-dollar-difference?all-topics/.

Farrer, Laurel. "Future of Education and Future of Work—Do They Match?" *Forbes.* April 30, 2019. https://www.forbes.com/sites/laurelfarrer/2019/04/30/future-of-education-and-future-of-work-do-they-match/#1d75984c79f0.

Kane, Karen, Russell Pearlman, and Hazel Euan-Smith. "The Very Human Future of Work." *Korn Ferry.* Accessed March 9, 2020. https://www.kornferry.com/insights/articles/2030-the-very-human-future-of-work/.

Kasriel, Stephane. "Skill, re-skill and re-skill again. How to keep up with the future of work." World Economic Forum, July 31, 2017. https://www.weforum.org/agenda/2017/07/skill-reskill-prepare-for-future-of-work/.

Kasriel, Stephane. "4 predictions for the future of work." World Economic Forum, December 05, 2017. https://www.weforum.org/agenda/2017/12/predictions-for-freelance-work-education/.

Mineo, Liz. "Time to Fix American Education with Race-For-Space Resolve." *The Harvard Gazette.* April 10, 2020. https://news.harvard.edu/gazette/story/2020/04/the-pandemics-impact-on-education/.

"OECD Ilibrary | PISA 2018 Results (Volume I): What Students Know and Can Do." 2020. *Oecd-Ilibrary.Org.* https://www.oecd-ilibrary.org/education/pisa-2018-results-volume-i_5f07c754-en/.

Oldham, Cheryl. "The Evolution of the Skills Gap Requires 21st Century Solutions." *Forbes.* March 4, 2019. https://www.forbes.com/sites/gradsoflife/2019/03/04/to-end-the-ever-growing-skills-gap-employers-must-change-their-outdated-hiring-practices/#4e-49b1a02d16/.

Schwab, Klaus. "The Fourth Industrial Revolution: What It Means and How to Respond." *World Economic Forum,* January 14, 2016.

https://www.weforum.org/agenda/2016/01/the-fourth-industrial-revolution-what-it-means-and-how-to-respond/.

Vander Ark, Tom. "What is 21st Century Learning? How Do We Get More?" *Getting Smart.* October 8, 2019. https://www.getting-smart.com/2019/10/what-is-21st-century-learning-how-do-we-get-more/.

Zinshteyn, Mikhail. "How the skills gap is changing the degree path." *Education Dive*, February 17, 2020. https://www.educa-tiondive.com/news/how-the-skills-gap-is-changing-the-degree-path/572382/.

ACKNOWLEDGMENTS

I would like to thank the following people for their support in creating this book:

Eric Koester, for helping shape the narrative and direction of the book.
Angela Ivey, my developmental editor, who helped me find my voice and narrative arc.
Kim LaCoste, my marketing editor, who helped me get out of my own head and get back on track.
Brian Bies, for helping with the creative stuff that is beyond me.

To the following for sharing your ideas and thoughts in our chats and interviews:

Ann Parker, Senior Content Manager
Annette Harris, President & Founder, ShowUp! LLC
Ayesha Sethi, Founder Sethi Learning & Company
Blanca Arciniega, HR Generalist
DeMarcus A. Pegues, PhD
Hassen Hafiz, Supply Chain Expert
Hunter Haines, Senior Organization Development Consultant

Lisette Ruch, Founder
Logan Deyo, Entrepreneur
Merrilea Mayo, CEO Social Tech
Nadia Laubach, CCMP, PMP, Manager, Instructional Design
Miriam Paska, Digital Strategist
Robyn Russo, Professor of English Northern Virginia Community College
Saleema Vellani, Co-Founder Innovazing
Dr. Terri Horton, EdD, MBA, MA, SHRM-CP, PHR, HCS, SWP
Tom Vander Ark, CEO Getting Smart
Saleha Bholat, Associate Dean Northern Virginia Community College
Sherry Steeley, Associate Teaching Professor Georgetown University
Warren Wright, CEO Second Wave Learning
Yasemin Hocaoglu, Realtor

My early supporters:

Amina Makhdoom Lynch	Ayesha Afzal
Zahra Shahid	Nadia Laubach
Arfa Syed	Hunter Haines
Kulsum Hassan	Hassen Hafiz
Sarah Sarfaraz	Sarah Malik
Diana Katz	Lauren Arevalo
Lauren Skor	Omairah Iqbal
Annette Harris	Nina Ahmed
Serwat Pervaiz	Megan Kobzej
Judit Markarian	Jaime Kapadia
Aroosha Rana	Carol Khalil
Mike Teller	Maryam Qureshi

Jill Saperstein
Amber Khan
Qaiser Khan

Sharon Khan
Attiya Afzal
E Abraham